GLOBETROTTER™

Travel Guide

DELHI
JAIPUR AND AGRA

KAPKA KASSABOVA
AND SAGARIKA GHOSE

NEW
HOLLAND

NEW
HOLLAND

★★★ Highly recommended
★★ Recommended
★ See if you can

Third edition published in 2008
by New Holland Publishers (UK) Ltd
London • Cape Town • Sydney • Auckland
10 9 8 7 6 5 4 3 2 1

website: www.newhollandpublishers.com

Garfield House, 86 Edgware Road
London W2 2EA, United Kingdom

80 McKenzie Street
Cape Town 8001, South Africa

Unit 1, 66 Gibbes Street
Chatswood, NSW 2067, Australia

218 Lake Road, Northcote
Auckland, New Zealand

Distributed in the USA by
The Globe Pequot Press, Connecticut

Copyright © 2008 in text: Kapka Kassabova and
Sagarika Ghose
Copyright © 2008 in maps: Globetrotter Travel Maps
Copyright © 2008 in photographs:
Individual photographers as credited (right)
Copyright © 2008 New Holland Publishers (UK) Ltd

ISBN 978 1 84773 101 2

Publishing Manager: Thea Grobbelaar
DTP Cartographic Manager: Genené Hart
Editors: Thea Grobbelaar, Jacqueline de Villiers, Tarryn Berry
Picture Researchers: Shavonne Govender,
Colleen Abrahams
Design and DTP: Nicole Bannister, Lellyn Creamer
Cartographers: Reneé Spocter, Nicole Bannister
Consultant: Sunil Vaidyanathan
Reproduction by Hirt & Carter (Pty) Ltd, Cape Town
Printed and bound by Times Offset (M) Sdn. Bhd.,
Malaysia.

This guidebook has been written by independent
authors and updaters. The information therein represents
their impartial opinion, and neither they nor the publishers accept payment in return for including in the
book or writing more favourable reviews of any of the
establishments. Whilst every effort has been made to
ensure that this guidebook is as accurate and up to date
as possible, please be aware that the facts quoted are
subject to change, particularly the price of food, transport and accommodation. The Publisher accepts no
responsibility or liability for any loss, injury or inconve-
nience incurred by readers or travellers using this guide.

Keep us Current
Information in travel guides is apt to change, which is
why we regularly update our guides. We'd be grateful to
receive feedback if you've noted something we should
include in our updates. If you have new information,
please share it with us by writing to the Publishing
Manager, Globetrotter, at the office nearest to you
(addresses on this page). The most significant contribu-
tion to each new edition will receive a free copy of the
updated guide.

Photographic Credits:
Anders Blomqvist: pages 4, 7, 9, 10, 12, 13, 18, 24,
25, 26, 27, 28, 30, 38, 39, 41, 42, 43, 44, 45, 47,
52, 53, 56, 57, 62, 64, 67, 68, 70, 74, 75, 76, 77,
80, 83, 84, 85, 94,109, 110, 116, 117, 118, 119,
120; **Gerald Cubitt:** pages 6, 8, 106, 113; **Gallo
Images:** page 87; **Gallo Images/Anthony Cassidy:** title
page; **Gallo Images/Paul Harris:** page 88; **Hutchison
Library:** pages 21, 50, 72; **Hutchison Library/ Gail
Goodger:** page 115; **Hutchison Library/C. Maurice
Harvey:** page 95; **Hutchison Library/Andrew Hill:** page
20; **Hutchison Library/Christine Pemberton:** pages 14,
33, 111, 114; **Hutchison Library/Liba Taylor:** page 86;
International PhotoBank/Jeanetta Baker: pages 15, 36;
International PhotoBank/ Peter Baker: cover, pages 34,
46, 49, 55; **Warren Jacobs:** pages 92, 101, 112;
Caroline Jones: pages 19, 23, 29, 65, 71, 90, 97; **Haike
Manning:** pages 22, 60; **Fiona Nichols:** pages 16, 54,
73, 98, 99, 100, 102, 103; **Christine Osborne Photo
Library/C. Milne:** page 11; **Christine Osborne Photo
Library/J. Worker:** , page 37; **Richard Sale:** page 69;
Nicholas Sumner: page 51.

Cover: *The magnificent Taj Mahal.*
Title page: *Five women in festival costume.*

CONTENTS

1
Introducing Delhi, Jaipur and Agra

The **Golden Triangle** of India, made up of **Delhi** at the apex and **Jaipur** and **Agra** at the western and eastern extremities, lies in the heart of north India. It is a **land-locked** region enclosed by the **Himalaya mountains** to the north, the Great Indian or **Thar desert** to the west and the **Aravalli hills** to the south. To the east stretch the teeming fertile plains of the **River Ganges**, endlessly green with fields of wheat, sugar cane, mustard and lentils. Delhi is the capital of India and also has the status of a state. Jaipur is the capital of the state of **Rajasthan** and Agra is the seat of the **Taj Mahal** and an important industrial and tourist centre in the state of **Uttar Pradesh**.

Successive empires have flourished in and around the Golden Triangle, from the ancient civilization of **Mohenjo Daro** and **Harappa** (2500BC–1700BC) west of Rajasthan to the ancient city of **Indraprastha** (1450BC) in Delhi and the powerful Rajput principalities that now make up the state of Rajasthan. Home to no fewer than seven historic cities, Delhi became the capital of the mighty Mughal empire (1526–1858) in which Delhi, Jaipur and Agra were bustling centres of arts and politics. The Golden Triangle evolved in the early 20th century with the arrival of the British; only Jaipur remained a semi-independent principality.

With Independence in 1947, the Golden Triangle became a crucible of politics. During the **freedom struggle**, Uttar Pradesh was the centre of powerful Gandhian movements and after Independence the majority of India's prime ministers came from that state. Modern-day Jaipur,

Opposite: *Elephant at Amber Fort-Palace.*

subsumed into the new country along with the rest of Rajasthan, is a shadow of its former glory, but nonetheless remains far more than an '**open air museum**' that shows off the art and architecture of the once-powerful Rajput kingdoms. Delhi's position as India's capital makes it a showcase for the country's richly layered history and society. The seven cities of Delhi (some say 15) make up a long chain of historic urban centres, of which New Delhi – built by the British between 1911 and 1939 – is the most recent. However, the current rapid expansion of Gurgaon south of the city could herald the arrival of the next.

The Golden Triangle is at a cultural vantage point between Hindu, Muslim and Western religions. The traditional and the modern face each other on every noisy colourful street corner. Muslim and Hindu, upper caste and gypsy swarm down the streets and into holy places. Opel Astras and bullock-carts pause together at traffic lights. Jean-clad young professionals climb up temple stairs. A caparisoned elephant might be brought in to celebrate the launch of a new software company, while the call of the muezzin competes with Hindu bells.

THE LAND

Below: *A typical street scene in Old Delhi, bustling with taxis and rickshaws.*

Every invader or traveller who galloped into India through the high passes in the northwest frontier, passed through this area and it is strategically vital for the control of the rich **Gangetic plain** as well as access to the trade routes of the **Gulf of Kutch**. Rajasthan is rugged terrain. The shifting sands of the desert are set aflame by the sun during the day and at night the clear desert air provides a magnificent view of the stars. Western Rajasthan is the *maru* or desert, but eastern Rajasthan is fertile with irrigated valleys that are home to the cities of Jaipur and the lake city of **Udaipur**. Delhi is situated on the banks of

the **Yamuna River**, a tributary of the Ganges, and lies roughly in the centre of north India. It is bordered by the Aravalli mountain ranges in the south with a shaky backbone, called the **North Ridge**, extending to the north. 223km (139 miles) from Delhi lies Agra, the capital of the Mughal empire from 1526 to 1648. Agra is also situated on the

banks of the Yamuna and is surrounded by the agricultural land known as the *braj-bhumi* (the ancient birthplace of the Hindu god Krishna). The towns of **Vrindavan** and **Mathura**, situated in the *braj*, are places of Hindu pilgrimage. The lush green of the Yamuna, south and west past Agra, gives way to the hot stony ravines of the **River Chambal**. This staggering landscape was once *dacoit* (gang) country. After the decline of the Mughals small kingdoms emerged here.

Above: *The Yamuna River runs through Delhi.*

Flora and Fauna

Many varieties of flowers bloom throughout the summer monsoon: there are among others marigold, begonias, chrysanthemums, poinsettias, nasturtiums, phlox and calendulas. New Delhi is lined with trees, such as tamarind, *amalta* (yellow-flowering), *neem* (medicinal), *jamun* (a tree with black berries) and *peepul* (a tree with large leaves useful for shade). Fluttering in Delhi's parks are many birds, such as sparrows, crows, kites, parrots, pigeons, as well as the grey hornbills, lapwings, babblers, *mynahs*, *papeehas* and *koels* (song birds), tree pies, magpie robins and golden orioles.

Occasionally, Delhi's streets are dignified by a visiting camel or elephant from Jaipur – either for a grand wedding or a fair – plodding loftily among the groups of placidly confident cattle which graze on Delhi's traffic islands or curl up for a nap in the traffic flow.

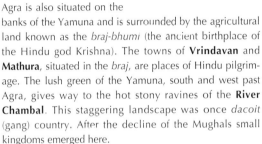

CLIMATE

Since the Golden Triangle is a landlocked area, the temperatures are extreme. In summer, particularly in May, June and July, the sun is ferocious and the heat is almost murderous, particularly when accompanied by the *loo*, a hot dry dust storm. In winter, notably December and January, the weather can turn quite cold and smoggy. The monsoon is usually unpredictable and can come any time between July and September. September is muggy and hot. The best time to visit the Golden Triangle is between October and March when the weather is cool and dry. January can be chilly and wet. February is the flowering month when the parks in Delhi and Agra begin to bloom. By March you can sense the onset of the great heat.

Above: *The tiger is a threatened species.*
Opposite: *From the Mahabharata: Krishna and Arjuna in battle.*

The **Sultanpur Bird Sanctuary**, 46km (29 miles) west of Delhi, is situated around a shallow *jheel* (lake). There are several pretty walks around it offering a sight of grandly flapping wings of the Sarus crane – the world's largest flying bird – or twinkling kingfishers.

Birds and animals were once the target for the hunting parties of sultans and viceroys. *Shikar* (hunting) was an important flourish of all India's rulers, whether Hindu, Islamic or British. Now, wildlife conservation initiatives like **Project Tiger** have resulted in strict laws on hunting. A famous film star was recently prosecuted for killing black buck. In the Golden Triangle you can see camels, elephants, the Siberian crane, the Nilgai deer, *sambhar*, spotted deer and tiger.

Bharatpur in eastern Rajasthan is renowned for the **Keoladeo Ghana National Park**, a former royal hunting preserve, which has been declared a world heritage site and is one of the world's best bird sanctuaries although now sadly under threat as its wetlands dry up. The name comes from a **Shiva temple** in a dense (*ghana*) forest. The park is spread over 29km² (11 square miles), and attracts over 375 bird species belonging to 56 families. Keoladeo is well worth a visit as a magnificent variety of birds can be seen, including the peregrine falcon, steppe eagle, garganey, teal and white ibis. Egrets, darters, cormorants, grey herons and storks hatch thousands of chicks here every year. The Siberian crane, now an endangered species, also migrates here. Wandering among the tall grass and wetlands of Keoladeo you can also see the Nilgai, the largest of the Asian deer, with their characteristic broad backs. At **Sariska National Park**, 107km (66 miles) from Jaipur and 200km (124 miles) from Delhi, you may be lucky enough to see a tiger during the day, although evenings are the best time to spot wildlife. You can also see tigers at **Ranthambhore National Park** near Bharatpur; there are about 45 tigers and a considerable bird population.

HISTORY IN BRIEF

The history of the Golden Triangle is also the story of the rise and fall of empires suffused with colourful local legends and folklore.

Through the ages, Delhi was a prize fought over by different empires. It remains a symbol of power for Indians. In fact, the rest of India, in a way, suffers from a 'Delhi complex'. If you talk to people in other cities in the south and east they will tell you how much they resent the pre-eminence of Delhi. But Delhi has been an important centre of political control and social change for at least five centuries.

The history of Delhi begins with the Hindu epic, the Mahabharata, which tells the story of five brothers – the Pandavas – who established a city called **Indraprastha** on the banks of the Yamuna in 1450BC. Since then seven – some say 15 – cities were built on this spot by **Rajputs**, **Turks** and the **Mughals**. The last city of Delhi was built by the British, but they ruled here for only 16 years.

Jaipur's story is part of the history of the Rajputs. It became the formal capital when the modern state of Rajasthan was formed after a long process of integration which began on 17 March 1948 and ended on 1 November 1956. The Rajputs of Rajasthan, or '**Rajputana**' as it was called then, were warrior clans who traced their descent from the sun and moon. They emerged in the sixth and seventh centuries and were such fierce fighters that no ruler of Delhi, be it Mughal or British, could ignore them. The relationship between the Rajputs and the Mughals is a long history of rebellion and then subsequent alliance. The rulers of **Jaipur** were the **Kachhawahas**, one of the Rajput warrior clans who settled in the Jaipur region and built the magnificent cities of **Amber** and **Jaipur**.

THE RAJPUTS

The Rajputs are believed to have emerged in the 6th and 7th centuries AD. They trace their descent from the sun and the moon and are divided into several warrior clans. They are like the knights of medieval Europe. They pride themselves on their gallantry, honour and chivalry. The Rajputs carved out kingdoms in the Rajasthan region and certain clans came to be associated with particular towns, such as the Kachhawaha clan of Jaipur. Today, the Rajputs run luxury hotels in Rajasthan or sit in parliament, but ask any Rajput and he will tell you of the valiant heritage of his family and how they stood up to all their foes. Their surnames are generally Singh (like the Sikhs) and although they never have beards they do, on occasion, sport a huge handlebar moustache!

अर्जुन को गीता का उपदेश   देते हुए श्री कृष्ण

Below: *Shah Jahan and Mumtaz Mahal, the story behind the Taj Mahal.*

Agra, imperial capital of Mughal rulers like Babur, Akbar and Jahangir, reflects the splendour of the Mughals, emperors so powerful, rich and grand that they have given the name, mogul, to Hollywood's mega film producers. The Mughals patronized the arts, music, garden design, jewellery and even cooking, and were tolerant of other religions. The city of Vrindavan (forest of fragrant basil) became an important pilgrim centre during Mughal rule when Chaitanya Mahaprabhu revived the Krishna cult. In addition to the splendid mosques and tombs of the Mughals – of which the Taj Mahal is the best example – the Golden Triangle also offers a historical aspect in the form of several important Hindu temples. For centuries, Muslims and Hindus co-existed here in relative peace, while Akbar went as far as marrying a Muslim, a Hindu and a Christian and forming his own new hybrid religion, Din-i-Ilahi.

Muslim Invasions

The first Islamic 'invaders' of India were the Turks. **Mahmud of Ghazni**, a conqueror from Kabul, raided India many times, including the rich temple of Somnath. After his death in 1033, **Mohammad Ghori** from Afghanistan raced into India and carved out an empire. After Ghori's death, **Qutab-ud-din-Aibak** became the first Sultan of Delhi. In the 12th century Aibak defeated the local Rajput ruler, **Prithviraj Chauhan**, and established the **Delhi Sultanate**. This famous defeat of 1191 has been described in Indian poems and songs and was the first event to begin the long reign of the central Asians over parts of India.

Five dynasties of Sultans made up the **Sultanate**: the **slaves**, the **khalji**, the **tughluqs**, the **sayyids** and the **lodis**. They ruled between 1206 and 1526, before the last Lodi Sultan was defeated at the famous **Battle of Panipat** in **1526** by the colourful

Turkish conqueror **Babur of Farghana**. During the time of the Sultanate, the **Turks** and **Rajputs** formed rival bases of power, the Turks in the area around Delhi and the Rajputs in the area of Rajputana. The Rajputs were divided into 36 houses or clans such as the **Mewar**, **Marwar** and **Amber**.

The Great Mughal Empire

The reasons for this conflict between Rajputs and the rulers of Delhi was trade. Every ruler of north India needed to have access to the **Gulf of Kutch** which opened the **sea route** to west Asia. The fertile soil of Gujarat in the west produced a rich cotton crop which was extremely valuable, but from the plains of north India access to Kutch and Gujarat lay through Rajputana. To secure this route, the sultans had to wage war with the Rajputs and for 350 years the two sides remained locked in battle. They were finally defeated in **1527** at the **Battle of Khanua** by the Mughals and never again united under a single banner. After Khanua, a number of shrewd Rajput houses sought alliances with the Delhi rulers. The height of the alliance was reached in the reign of the far-sighted Mughal emperor **Akbar** (1556–1605) who co-opted the powerful Rajput princes into the Mughal ruling system.

Babur was the founder of the Mughal dynasty in India. Of him, the British historian Lane-Poole writes, '*The blood of the two great scourges of Asia, **Timur the Lame** and **Ghengiz Khan** mixed in his veins and to the daring and restlessness of the nomad tartar, he joined the culture and urbanity of the Persian.*' Babur ruled from 1526–30. But it was his grandson who took the Mughal empire to glory.

Akbar inherited only a tiny piece of territory stretching between Delhi and Agra, and parts of Rajputana. But half a century later, he handed over to his son **Jahangir** a dominion that spanned from **Kabul** in the west to **Bengal** in the east, from **Kashmir** in the north to parts of the **Deccan** in the south. Akbar built a complicated and mighty state with the Golden Triangle at its core. He promulgated the doctrine of

Above: *A memorial to Rajiv Gandhi, adorned with a marigold lei.*

THE UNTOUCHABLES

The Untouchables or *dalits* were at the very bottom of the Indian social ladder. There are about 170 million *dalits* in India today, still subject to horrifying discrimination. In villages, they are assigned segregated areas to build their homes. Untouchables were called *harijans* or 'children of god' by Gandhi who campaigned for their rights all his life. Traditionally, the Untouchables cleaned people's toilets. Their presence was regarded as 'polluting' by all Hindus, and some orthodox Hindus used to bathe if an untouchable's shadow fell on them. After independence, 22.5% of the seats in Parliament were reserved for Untouchables. Today, *dalits* are becoming ministers and even president of India. However most *dalits* continue to be extremely poor and illiterate.

Right: *Akbar's impressive tomb in Sikandra.*
Opposite: *A portrait of the liberal Mughal Emperor Akbar.*

sulh-i-kul (peace to all) a civic religion which teaches personal religion as being subsumed in a higher duty to the state and government. Presiding over an empire with vast differences in religious beliefs, Akbar created an overarching umbrella that gave the empire a pluralist face. As part of his strategy of co-option he invited the Rajput nobility into the ruling elite.

Akbar is regarded as one of the great statesmen of India. The Rajputs bowed to him. **Raja Bhara Mal** of Amber realized that the Mughals were too powerful to fight and concluded an alliance with them. Raja Man Singh, Bhara Mal's grandson, became one of Akbar's most trusted lieutenants. Akbar even married a Rajput princess, **Jodhai Bai**. Only the House of Mewar continued to resist the Mughals.

The history of the Rajput house of **Mewar** in Rajputana, with its capital at **Chittor** and its three rulers **Rana Kumbha**, **Rana Sunga** and **Rana Pratap**, illustrates the legendary valour of the Rajputs as well as their fierce attachment to honour and self-sacrifice. *Jauhar* (or the practise of self-immolation) is when a queen jumped into a funeral pyre if her prince had been defeated in battle and *sati* is when a widow jumps (or is helped) into the funeral pyre with her dead husband. Although strictly illegal, *sati* is practised even today. The beautiful queen **Padmini of Mewar** is said to have committed *jauhar* when her husband **Rattan Singh** was defeated by **Sultan Alauddin Khilji** early in the 14th century. Rana Pratap's name is synonymous in Indian

HISTORICAL CALENDAR

2500–1500BC Indus Valley civilization in northwest India.
321–185BC Maurya Dynasty founded by Chandragupta; his grandson Ashoka becomes India's first emperor, ruling from Delhi.
AD1–400s Huge Hindu empires.
8th–11th centuries Rajputs arrive from west, followed by first Muslim invasions of India.
11th–12th centuries Turks conquer north India, leaving governors to rule. They break away and form the Delhi Sultanate.
1526 Babur defeats the Sultan of Delhi at the Battle of Paniput.
1526–1707 Great Mughal Empire – a golden era for arts, literature and architecture.

1612 First British trading post established in Surat by the East India Company.
1757 Battle of Plassey, the British conquer Bengal.
Early 1800s The East India Company becomes a political power in India.
1857 Sepoy Mutiny.
1858 India becomes part of the British Empire.
1885 Formation of the Indian National Congress.
1915 Mohandas Karamchand Gandhi arrives in India from South Africa and leads the independence movement.
1947 Independence and the partition of India.
1948 Gandhi is assassinated.
1949 Maharajahs agree to join 23 principalities to India,

creating Rajasthan.
1950 India's first constitution.
1975 Prime Minister Indira Gandhi imposes the emergency.
1991 Free market reforms are introduced.
1999 Conflict with Pakistan over Kashmir.
2001 Severe earthquake hits Gujarat, killing 20,000 people.
July 2002 APJ Abdul Kalam is elected president.
May 2004 Manmohan Singh is sworn in as prime minister.
March 2006 USA and India sign a nuclear agreement during a visit by US President George W Bush.
May 2007 Government announces strongest economic growth figures for 20 years – 9.4% in the year to March.

history with bravery and defiance of Delhi's rule. Pratap was the only Rajput whom even Akbar could not subdue for a long time, although he was finally defeated at the famous **Battle of Haldighati** in 1576. There were Mughal 'emperors' right up to the time of the 1857 Indian Uprising, although they did not have an empire.

The British in India

By the 17th century the **British** had arrived in India. The **East India Company** established major ports at Madras and Calcutta in the east, and Surat and Bombay in the west. In 1614, **Sir Thomas Roe**, envoy of **James I**, had arrived at the court of Jahangir offering to negotiate a trading agreement between the Mughal empire and the Company. Soon the British, taking advantage of feuds between Indian rulers and the decline of the Mughals, had become an influential political

A GREAT SOUL

Mohandas Karamchand Gandhi was not a simple man. Born in 1869, he was the son of the hereditary Prime Minister of Kathiawar, trained as a barrister in London and moved to South Africa, where his political career was jump-started by the racism he encountered. He returned to India in 1915, launched the first campaign of civil disobedience in 1920, and by 1921 had adopted the signature white *dhoti* (loincloth) worn by the untouchables. His powerful civil protests and spiritual leadership worked with the more overtly political Nehru to achieve Indian independence. He was assassinated by a Hindu extremist in Delhi in 1948.

Below: *Coronation Park is a resting place of old British Statues, George V on the left.*

force. In 1774 **Warren Hastings** became the first governor general of British India.

By the 18th century Mughal power, which had seen eruption under Akbar and his grandson **Shah Jahan** (builder of the Taj Mahal), had begun to wane. The last Great Mughal, **Aurangzeb**, presided over a stretched empire, increasingly vulnerable to blood feuds between rival claimants to the throne. Aurangzeb, a cruel, autocratic ruler, murdered his older brother **Dara Shikoh** and imprisoned his father Shah Jahan to acquire the throne. The empire was now under attack from the **Marathas**, a sturdy band of warriors from western India. The Marathas had also been plundering the Rajput kingdoms. In desperation the princes turned to the British. In the early 19th century, the house of Jaipur made an alliance with the British. They signed treaties giving up their independence in return for British protection. Other Rajput houses followed suit and **British residents** were installed in the Rajput palaces. The British also conquered Delhi and Agra at the same time.

The Mughal empire was now in a pathetic state, reduced to the precincts of the **Red Fort** in Delhi. The later Mughals were weak rulers and the last Mughal emperor's name has become a byword of political decline in modern India. His name is **Bahadur Shah Zafar** and he died, in 1862 in **Burma**, in exile, blind and without an empire.

Independence

In 1857 the British faced a crucial test. The **War of Independence** (Bengal Rebellion or **Sepoy Mutiny of 1857**) was a turning point for the British empire in India. A rumour spread that the bullets issued to soldiers were greased with pig or cow fat. All across north India, Hindu and Muslim sepoys rose against the rule of the

Company, followed by many others. **Rani Laxmibai of Jhansi**, warrior queen and accomplished equestrian, became famous at this time. The uprising was finally crushed by a small British force led by the heroic **Brigadier General Nicholson** who died in battle. In 1858 India was placed under the direct governorship of the Crown and Victoria became an empress. In 1911, at the famous **Delhi Durbar**, **George V** announced to an audience of 561 maharajahs and a dazzling display of elephants, jewels and Rolls Royce cars that the capital of India was to be shifted from Calcutta to New Delhi.

A few years later the Indian freedom struggle began in earnest. The **Indian National Congress** had already been formed in 1885. In 1915 **Mohandas Karamchand Gandhi** (or *Mahatma*, meaning Great Soul) arrived in India from **South Africa**. By 1920 Gandhi had become the supreme symbol of the Indian freedom struggle. Travelling third class, speaking simple Hindi and wearing only a loin cloth, he converted the freedom movement from a genteel group of upper class negotiators – most of them lawyers educated in England – to a massive passionate movement across India. Thousands joined his movement of *satyagraha* (war for truth) and *ahimsa* or non-violent protest. Huge political movements like the Non-Cooperation agitation of 1922 or the **Civil Disobedience** of 1932 and the **Quit India movement** of 1942 took place under the leadership of Gandhi, Nehru and the Congress Party. In 1945 the Labour govern-

Above: *Mahatma Gandhi, leader of a nation.*

THE EUNUCHS OF INDIA

The eunuchs or transvestites of India, known as *hijras*, are unique and at an estimated half a million, form a substantive, and ancient, subculture and a caste of their own. You may see them in the streets of Old Delhi, in Lodi Gardens on weekends – or indeed in any other city. They dress as women and some look quite feminine, while others have decidedly male features and body-shapes. Traditionally, the eunuchs were highly valued at the royal courts of the Mughals and were exclusive harem-guardians, often reaching positions of power. The curse of a *hijra* is still widely feared – which is why they make their living from dancing and singing at weddings and births. Many *hijras* are forced to take up prostitution.

Above: *Buildings of the Secretariat, New Delhi.*

ment was elected to power in Britain and preparations for handing over independence to India began. On 14 August 1947 the last Viceroy of India, **Lord Mountbatten**, handed over power to the Indian National Congress. India was partitioned, Pakistan was created and Delhi became the capital of independent India. The first prime minister, **Jawaharlal Nehru** made his famous speech about India's '**tryst** with **destiny**' from the ramparts of the Red Fort in Delhi. The freedom movement has been greatly mythologized in modern India and this emotional speech is taught in every school across the country.

The independence and partition of India and the subsequent creation of Pakistan saw unprecedented **religious riots** and **mass killings**. As soon as the new borders were announced, 10 million Hindus, Muslims and Sikhs fled from their homes in India and Pakistan. Around one million died fighting. In the same year, the state of Jammu and Kashmir was invaded by Pakistani forces. Thus began the long and blood-stained dispute over **Kashmir** between India and Pakistan that continues to take a heavy toll of human life to this day. On 30 January 1948 a Hindu fundamentalist shot and killed Gandhi. With the great leader died his treasured politics of non-violence.

GOVERNMENT AND ECONOMY

India is the world's largest democracy where even the poorest and the illiterate have a vote. While this gives hope to many, it has also led to some peculiar Indian practices such as the emergence of 'vote banks', or enclaves of voters who vote according to ethnic or community loyalties, and the increasing importance of **caste** as a means of political organization. Today, caste identities are very important in politics as castes often vote as a group.

HAWKERS

Particularly numerous, noisy and tiring in tourist areas, hawkers try to sell cheap kitsch to tourists. If you wish to buy a miniature plastic Taj Mahal, a toy snake, or bangles, make it clear that you are only purchasing this particular item, otherwise you might be trampled by other hopefuls. If you wish to buy, bargain hard. If you do not wish to buy anything, make that clear, too, by saying 'No, thank you' politely, but emphatically. They will pursue you until you get the message across or until they find another victim and lose interest in you.

India's democracy is robust and colourful and although there has been a ban on loud speakers and decorations during elections since 1996, a carnival atmosphere pervades at this time. Astrologers, wrestlers, folk dancers and street performers are all roped in to further electoral fortunes. Incidents of violence, **booth capturing** and **proxy voting** are also common.

The transportation of ballot boxes from remote areas to counting centres has in the past been the subject of many photo-essays. Ballot boxes were transported on the backs of elephants or by boat, or by camel-drawn carts through the desert to reach remote villages in the interior. Nowadays ballot boxes are obsolete and electronic voting machines (EVMs) are used.

The Indian Constitution, announcing a **Sovereign**, **Secular**, **Socialist Republic** came into force in 1950. The event is celebrated every year with grand Republic Day parades in all major cities, generally showing off India's military might and floats of its traditional culture. The president is the head of state, the prime minister is the head of government. There is a two-house parliament. The *Lok Sabha* is the House of the People with 545 seats. The *Rajya Sabha* is the Council of States with 250 seats. Every state capital follows the same structure with a *Vidhan Sabha* (Lower House) and a *Vidhan Parishad* (Upper House). Most of the larger Indian villages have village councils known as *panchayats*. The panchayat is often the arena where a number of politicians cut their teeth before they can contest state elections. If they are popular enough, they are given tickets for the national elections. The politician-criminal nexus or role of thuggery and corruption is high in the Indian political scene where some candidates even contest election from prison.

GOVERNMENT

India is a **socialist** and **secular** republic with 28 states and 7 union territories. The government of India is a federation of **democratically elected** state governments. Head of State is the **president**, but political control resides with the **prime minister**, appointed by members of the majority parliamentary party. This is currently the Congress Party, closely followed by the BJP (Bharatiya Janata Party). The President is Pratibha Patil (the first female president of India), the Prime Minister, Manmohan Singh.

Below: *The dream of independence, India's first national flag.*

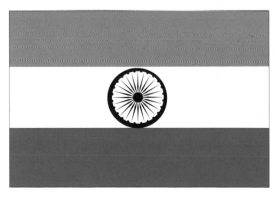

Below: *Jawaharlal Nehru, the first Prime Minister.*

Jawaharlal Nehru, the first prime minister, died in 1964 and was replaced by **Lal Bahadur Shastri**. When Shastri died, Nehru's daughter, **Indira Gandhi**, who is criticized for being autocratic and not as visionary as her father, was elected to succeed him. The Congress party split in 1969, and Indira Gandhi became leader of the Congress. She declared the **Emergency** in 1975, was ousted in 1977 and won a landslide victory in 1980. She was gunned down by her Sikh bodyguards in 1984 after she ordered the controversial storming of the **Sikh** religious **shrine**, the Golden Temple. Riding a huge sympathy wave, her son **Rajiv Gandhi** swept the polls in the largest mandate in Indian history, but lost the 1989 elections to **VP Singh** after scandals regarding the purchase of the Bofors gun from a Swedish company. Singh commissioned the infamous **Mandal Commission Report** allowing the reservation of government jobs for those classified as backward castes. This report set in motion a movement of the assertion of backward caste demands, which is becoming ever more powerful today. In 1990, **Chandrashekhar** replaced Singh. In the run-up to the 10th general elections, Rajiv Gandhi was assassinated by a **Tamil suicide bomber** as a result of his having ordered an **Indian Peace Keeping Force** to intervene in the civil war between Tamils and Sinhalas in **Sri Lanka**. After Rajiv's death, the Congress Party limped to power and prime minister **PV Narasimha Rao** formed a minority Congress government.

In 1991 this government initiated the liberation of India's economy by starting to dismantle the socialist economy and introducing free-market reforms. After the 1996 elections the **Bharatiya Janata**, a broadly right-wing Hindu nationalist party, briefly formed a government, to be replaced by two others in quick succession lead by Deve Gowda and IK Gujral. In the 1999 elections, the Bharatiya Janata Party and its allies came into power.

The Bharatiya Janata Party (BJP) achieved

national prominence after the demolition of the **Babri Masjid** mosque in Ayodhya, said to stand on the site of a Rama temple, in 1992. Since then the BJP has been associated with majoritarian Hindu sentiments, an image it is now trying to live down by appealing to broader sections of the population. In recent years, the emergence of regional parties like the Telegu Desam of **Andhra Pradesh**,

Above: *Bicycle rickshaw at the Red Fort.*

Trinamool Congress in West Bengal and the **AIADMK** and **DMK** in Tamil Nadu have considerably blunted the power of the older national parties. However, in 2004, Congress Party regained power during the national elections, its campaign spearheaded by Rajiv Gandhi's charismatic Italian widow, Sonia. Most expected her to become prime minister and continue the Nehru dynasty, but she stepped aside in favour of Manmohan Singh.

Delhi is currently controlled by Congress, and Rajasthan by the BJP. The recent elections in Uttar Pradesh were a turning point in the politics of this most populous Indian state. The Dalit leader Mayawati of the Bahujan Samaj Party won a landslide victory against Mulayam Singh Yadav (Samajwadi Party) in a re-election after the government led by the latter was dissolved. This defeat is attributed to rampant corruption and bad governance during the tenure of the Samajwadi Party.

Left-wing structures like the **Communist Party of India** (CPI) and the **Communist Party of India [Marxist]** (CPI[M]) do not get too many votes but are influential lobbying and pressure groups.

Although Lucknow is state capital, Agra plays an important part in the politics of **Uttar Pradesh**, which is India's most politically significant state, as it sends the largest number of members to the parliament of the *Lok Sabha*.

The recent change in Uttar Pradesh's electoral trends contradicted the theory of caste being an indicator of

GHATS

Ritual bathing in holy water is an important part of Hindu belief. *Ghats* are steps that lead down into rivers or lakes and each one is given its own name. The word comes from the Hindi *ghati* which means valley. The stairs leading down into the water are seen as valleys leading into the river. The *ghats* that line the Ganges are considered spiritually important and a number of temples are situated along this river. Pilgrims descend these steps to bathe in the holy water and to take some home with them. You will also see *sadhus* meditating, smoking *ganja* (marijuana) or just praying to the sun rising above the river. Alarmingly, some are also used as cremation grounds, with ashes and even bodies then given to the sacred waters – amongst the bathers.

Above: *Republic Day celebrations at India Gate.*

electoral fortunes. The astute Mayawati had a simple but effective solution to the caste quandary; she gave election tickets to influentials from across the caste strata. Both Dalit and Brahmin rallied for her and led her to victory.

Rajasthan is a recent addition to the political map of India. It was only created in 1956, with Jaipur as its capital, when the privy purses of the princes were abolished. After the British left, their paramountcy over the princely states of Rajputana lapsed and the states were left technically free of all control and without relationship with the rest of India. The merging of all the little principalities of Rajputana took a long time and only after the strenuous efforts by the country's first home minister, **Sardar Vallabhai Patel**, did the princes agree to accept the sovereignty of independent India. The **maharajahs**, stripped of their riches and powers, are mute spectators to the new democracy. The present head of the Kachhawaha dynasty is **Maharajah Bhawani Singh** (or Bubbles, as he is called because of the amount of champagne drunk at the time of his birth). His father, **Man Singh II**, was one of the most anglicized of all Rajputs, and a keen collector of vintage cars. Many modern Rajput princes are educated, at least in part, in the UK.

Economy

Reforms to change the socialist-style planned economy were introduced in 1991. They generated huge increases in private investment and boosted exports and imports, but they were also inconsistent and created social unrest. The objective of the reforms was to reduce the role of the public sector in heavy manufacturing, banking, telecommunication and power generation, but there is still a long way to go. Today, fringe groups like the right-wing Swadeshi Jagran Manch as well as the left oppose economic reforms. Indian industrialists continue to demand a level playing field, ie. equal benefits for foreign and domestic companies.

India's main exports are **gems**, **jewellery**, **cotton yarn** and **fabrics**, **handicrafts**, **engineering goods**, **chemicals** and **leather goods**. The last few years have shown remarkable economic progress with real signs of prosperity and the government talking of overtaking the UK within 10 years. However, the huge numbers of people employed by the government are heavily unionized and resist any attempts at streamlining. Economists claim that reforms are taking place only in the big cities while the rest of the country remains consigned to agrarian backwardness.

Agriculture is no longer the main economic activity in India, contributing 23.4% to the Gross Domestic Product, although it employs 60% of the total workforce. India is the world's largest **milk producer** and, at 193 million, has among the largest number of cattle in the world. Cows can be seen wandering on every street in the country. India is the world's largest producer of rice and tea and the fourth largest of **wheat**. It is also a world leader in the **banana**, **mango**, **coconut** and **cashew** market, as well as that of **potatoes**, **tomatoes**, **onions** and **green peas**. It is also one of the world's 10 largest producers of **pineapples** and **apples**. Industry now accounts for 28.4% of GDP and 17% of the workforce. Services provide 48% of GDP although employing only 23% of workers.

The Golden Triangle is a relatively prosperous zone. Benetton, McDonald's and Pepsi outlets are mushrooming in the smaller towns of this region. In Rajasthan there are over 125,000 small-scale industries and over 200 large and medium-sized industries. Rajasthan has invested about 20 billion US dollars in the industrial sector. Delhi is an industrial hub and seat of many multinationals like Adobe, Coca Cola and Pepsi, including several international banks such as ABN Amro and Standard & Chartered Bank. The majority of Delhi's population has come here for economic reasons as the local average wage is double that paid in the rest of the country. Agra,

LANGUAGE

Hindi is the most widely spoken and understood of India's 15 official regional languages (with 65 subgroups). It belongs to the northern group of languages along with Bengali, Punjabi and Gujarati. Most Hindi speakers are concentrated in the Golden Triangle, especially in Delhi. English is one of the official languages, still commonly used as a neutral language of higher education and government.

Below: *Drying racks for freshly dyed saris.*

too, is situated in the more prosperous western Uttar Pradesh, a region which is home to industry and mechanized agriculture. The eastern part of Uttar Pradesh is poverty-stricken and very backward.

THE PEOPLE

As in the rest of India, the people of the Golden Triangle are a colourful mix of communities, religions, languages and traditional tribes. All the gradations of the caste system (see page 10) are found here: the upper *brahmins* and *kshatriyas*, the middle-ranking *vaishyas* and the lowest, menial labourers. Then there are the Untouchables (*dalits, see* panel, page 11), who do not have a caste and are the the lowest and poorest of them all. Almost all of India's communities are represented in Delhi: **Tamils** and **Keralites**, **Punjabis**, **Bengalis**, as well as **Maharashtrians**, **Gujaratis** and students from the northeastern states of **Assam** and **Nagaland**.

It is interesting to see how certain communities have created their own housing areas in the capital. **Janak Puri** in west Delhi is dominated by Keralites and Tamils, while **Chittaranjan Park** in south Delhi is made up almost entirely by Bengalis. It is complete with a market that stocks a wide variety of delicious fish.

Thousands of migrant labourers from the villages of Bihar, Uttar Pradesh and Haryana swarm into Delhi to look for work. Certain jobs and services have become associated with distinct communities and castes. **Tribal Christian girls** from Bihar work as housemaids, a number of plumbers come from **Orissa**, the nurses from **Kerala**, and the *dosa* (south Indian bread) restaurants are, of course, all staffed by Tamils or Keralites.

Below: *Smiling children in Jaipur reflect the origins of their forefathers.*

In Delhi, you can also see the **puppie**, or Punjabi Upwardly Mobile Professional, zoom by in a Hyundai or Honda and swing in some of the city's booming nightclubs. India's **Generation X** are called the **trendy conservatives**. They dress fashionably and listen to the latest western pop music, but few are able to break out of parental control. Living together, having gay relationships and even divorce are still fairly unacceptable.

In Rajasthan the most visible group are the Rajputs – the warriors representing different noble houses – like the Kachhawahas of Jaipur, the Rathods of Jodhpur and the Sisodias of Mewar. Together with the *brahmins* they constitute less than a tenth of Rajasthan's population. With a brightly coloured turban and handlebar moustache, the Rajput prides himself on his ancestry, although many have now fallen on hard times and have been forced to convert their ancestral properties into luxury hotels. Rajput villagers might be tall and brightly turbaned, but they are also impoverished and skinny.

There are several other communities like the **Marwaris** (traditional traders). One of India's richest industrialist families, the Birlas, are Marwaris. There are tribes like the **Bishnois**, traditional conservationists who have been known to commit suicide in their efforts to protect trees and animals. There are also *banjaras* (gypsies) who wear colourful clothes and **heavily oxidized silver jewellery**. In fact, the highly skilled artisans of Rajasthan are becoming leading couturiers. Their vibrantly coloured **mirror-work fabric**, block-prints, silver jewellery set with semi-precious stones, ornament design and *minakari* jewellery (mirrorwork on gold), as well as *bandhani* print (the tie and dye print, patterned with tiny white squares, circles and lines) are justifiably famous. Most of India's artisans have been practising their art for generations

Above: *Jaipur City Palace guards with characteristic brightly coloured Rajasthani turbans.*

LITERACY

Approximately 68.5% of India is literate – 70.2% of men are literate but only 48.3% of women can read and write. Delhi's literacy rate is 79%. Indians love politics, and political discussions are loudly carried out in *baithaks* (gatherings), *chai* (tea) stalls and roadside *dhabas* (snack stalls). No wonder then that there are around 1800 daily newspapers and an explosion of interest in the Internet and satellite TV.

Above: *The Elephant Festival in Jaipur is one of the best in India.*

and some, like the celebrated *minakars* (jewellery artisans) of Jaipur trace their descent as far back as the 17th century.

Agra has almost the same social landscape as Delhi where Hindu and Muslim have lived as friendly neighbours (and occasional enemies) for centuries. The Agra region is not only known for its Islamic monuments, but also for the Hindu Krishna cult that flourishes around Vrindavan, an important Hindu pilgrim centre north of Agra.

Hindus generally believe in the two epics, (*Ramayana* and *Mahabharata)*, the fact that all living beings are manifestations of the Supreme Being or *brahman* and that there are three aspects to God: **Creator** (*Brahma*), **Destroyer** (*Shiva*) and **Preserver** (*Vishnu*). But there are also a huge number of local gods, small shrines and cults, all of which are recognized as Hindu if they are associated with the holy trinity or the two epics.

Muslims believe in the Prophet Muhammad's teachings as set down in their holy book, the Qur'an. In India, the **Sufi** or mystical aspects of Islam are also strong. The Sufi (wandering mystic) is known for his personal communion with God. He whirls in ecstasy while praying and is known as a *mast qalandar* (intoxicated by devotion). The shrine of **Khwaja Moinuddin Chisti** in Ajmer is an important centre for the Islamic world. The **Sikhs**, with their main shrine at the Golden Temple in Amritsar, believe in the teachings of their gurus, while **Buddhism** and **Jainism** adhere to doctrines of compassion, non-violence and personal communion with God. They are systems of philosophy and codes of morality that adhere to the achievement of enlightenment.

Food and Drink

North Indian cuisine is generally called *mughlai* food with a heavy emphasis on barbecued and curried meats and

---

FOOD TERMS

badam • almond
dhal • lentils
dosa • crispy rice-pancake
ghee • clarified butter
gulab jamun • fried Bengali sweet soaked in syrup
iddli • steamed rice cake
lassi • fresh yoghurt drink (salted or sweetened)
masala • spices
naan • leavened bread made with yoghurt
roti • general term for tandoor-baked bread
tandoor • clay oven
thali • an all-in-one meal: a platter of vegetarian or non-vegetarian dishes, pickles, rice and bread

breads and rice eaten with flavoured yoghurt. A vegetable or non-vegetable *thali* (a metal dish) set with metal *katoris* (bowls), is a full Indian meal consisting of rice, bread, curries, chutneys, *papads* (crispy deep fried wafers), curds and *mithai* (generic term for Indian sweets). *Biryani* (rice flavoured with spices and cooked with chunks of meat or vegetables) and *pulao* (rice mixed with vegetables, lamb or chicken) are also common. Typical vegetable dishes are *sabzi* (mixed vegetable), *baigan bharta* (curried eggplant) and *aloo jeera* (spiced potatoes). Standard non-vegetarian dishes would be butter chicken, *rogan josh* (lamb curry), *gushtaba* (meatballs) or chicken *korma* (curry with curd). *Kebabs* (skewered barbecued meats) are common in Delhi, as are *shammi* (flat kebabs of minced meat), *seekh* (sausages of seasoned lamb) and *burra* (pieces of lamb grilled on a charcoal fire).

Communities like the **Jains** and certain *brahmins* are strict vegetarians. Typical south Indian fare like *dosas* (rice pancakes), *idlis* (steamed rice dumplings) and *sambhar* (savoury lentils) is also completely vegetarian and available all over Delhi and Agra. Roadside stalls dispense cut fruit, *samosas* (fried and stuffed dumplings), *paapri chaat* (savoury pastry chips smothered in curds and chutney) and *chole bhatoore* (spiced chickpeas with fried bread), but these are best avoided. **Delhi belly** (food or water poisoning) can sometimes turn nasty and even locals suffer if they are not careful. *Mithai* (sweets), made from thickened milk and sugar are generally safe. Different types of *mithai* are: *laddoos* (sweet yellow balls), *jalebis* (twisted fried sugar), *gulab jamuns* (cardamom-flavoured caramelized sugar-and-milk balls) and *kulfi* (ice cream).

Dhal (lentils) and cereal (rice or bread) is the staple diet all across this region. Most Indians eat *achar* (pickles) with their meals. Other side dishes include *dahi* (curd) or *raita*

PAAN

You will see people -- mostly men -- chewing and spitting a blood-coloured substance in the streets. This is produced from chopped betel nut, a mild hallucinogen, with various additives such as white lime, *mitha masala* (sweet spices) and *zarda* (chewing tobacco, which is not to be swallowed), wrapped in a betel leaf. *Paan* is sold in square foil at countless street stalls. For first-time users, the *mitha* variety is recommended as it can safely be ingested. Indians can spit *paan* juice from a mile, sometimes leading the visitor to think they are vomiting blood. A certain type of *paan* is known as the *palang-tod* (wrecker of beds), since it supposedly acts as an aphrodisiac.

Below: *Making* naan *in a traditional* tandoor *oven.*

(flavoured curd with cucumber or tomatoes). A common drink is *lassi* or iced yoghurt shake. Indian beer is high in alcohol content and brands like **Kingfisher** and **Haake Beck** are good. Try to avoid brands like **Thunderbolt** that have a ferociously high alcohol content. Many restaurants do not serve alcohol.

Architecture

The architecture of the Golden Triangle is grand and there are monuments here in the **Hindu**, **Indo-Islamic** and **British colonial** styles.

The Indo-Islamic style is evident in the **Taj Mahal** (*see* page 96) and the other elegant luxuriously carved monuments in Agra. The Taj (proud passion of an Emperor's love) is a beautiful, melancholic monument built by **Shah Jahan**. This Mughal emperor was so devoted to his wife **Mumtaz Mahal**, who died in delivering her child, that he built this memorial to her. Legend has it that the emperor had the thumbs of all the artisans cut off after they finished their breathtaking carvings, so that they would never be able to build another like it ever again. The Mughals used a great deal of **white marble** and **red sandstone** and the Taj is the best example of Mughal style with its elegant minarets and dome, elevated platform, rich carvings and screens.

The decorated forts, tombs and gardens of Agra show Mughal splendour at its height. The *pietra dura* technique (inlaid flowery patterns of semi-precious stones on marble) can also be seen here, as well as the use of running water for cooling. The delicate **Itimad-ud-Daulah's Tomb** in Agra (*see* page 103) is described as a 'jewelbox of marble' and is, to some, even more beautiful than the Taj itself.

The red sandstone desert palace **fortresses** of Rajasthan show the varied styles used by Rajput architects. They are

Below: *Delicious* mithai *are made from thickened milk, sugar and flavouring.*

decorated with carved wooden doors, balconies, pillared verandas, mirrors and mosaics, latticed windows, *chhatris* (pavilions), painted walls, tall battlements and domes in the Mughal style. The colonial buildings erected by the British in **Delhi** use a combination of classical western and Indian styles and they are indisputable reminders that this was the capital of British India. There is an interesting area, north of the old city, known as **Civil Lines** where the British used to live.

The geometrically designed **Jaipur** (also known as the Pink City) and the **Jantar Mantar** observatory show the modernism of Jaipur's remarkable founder **Sawai Jai Singh II**.

Modern Indian architecture is higgledy piggledy, with all manner of styles and constructions juxtaposed on each other. The luxury villas in Delhi and Jaipur are as fanciful as their owners want them to be. Those with the money to build big houses are not too bothered about history. The restoration of old buildings is sadly neglected and beautiful old *havelis* (townhouses) in Old Delhi have been allowed to fall into ruin. Old and new are combined curiously. Chrome-and-glass high-rises stretch glossily behind Lutyens's (the chief architect of New Delhi) colonial buildings. The clamour and traffic of Jaipur obscures its meticulously planned structure.

Above: *Floral motif in multicoloured marble, in the Taj Mahal.*

Crafts

North Indian crafts range from delicate embroidery on cotton to textile design and intricate jewellery manufacture, as well as folk art such as puppet making and creating clay idols for festivals. Agra is renowned for its gold thread and bead embroidery known as *zardozi* and the *pietra dura* stonework handed down through families since the 17th century. Agra is also the centre of the old Mughal imperial carpet works. Fine carpets are made both here and in Jaipur.

The *karigars* (craftsmen) of Jaipur are proud, skilled artists who have perfected their art over centuries. Textile design is a specialty of the region. The *bandhani* workers,

ARCHITECTURAL GLOSSARY

bagh • garden
chhatri • cenotaph, tomb/domed pavilion
chowk • square, crossroads
diwan • hall
ghat • steps to a river
gurdwara • Sikh temple
hammam • bath-house
haveli • townhouse with courtyard
jaali • latticed stone or marble screen
mandir • Hindu temple
masjid • mosque
pol • fort gate
zenana • women's quarters (Hindu)

mostly women, transfer designs onto cotton or chiffon by tying yards of cloth. The *ghagra* (flaring skirt), *choli* (short tied top) and *odhni* (veil) make up the typical Rajasthani dress. In Jaipur, shops like **Anokhi** stock typical block-printed cottons. In fact, its owner, Faith Singh, an English-woman by birth, has helped to sell the hand- and block-printed designs (*chhapai*) to tourists and internationally. The owners of the popular shop **Fabindia** in Delhi have done the same. It is easy, quick and cheap to get clothes made in cotton or silk as long as you can provide a template to copy.

Jaipur is also the largest ornament-production centre in India and the expert artisans here work on *zari* (silver and gold thread fabric) and *gota* (gold thread material). Emerald design, garnet-setting, stone-cutting, wood-carving as well as the highly skilled *minakari* (enamelled jewellery work) in which tiny pieces of glass are fused on gold, are all practised in Jaipur. Between them, the towns of **Sanganer**, **Barmer** and **Bagru** in Rajasthan produce about 250,000m (275,000 yards) of printed fabric every day. The **Sanganeri** print is very famous, as is Rajasthani silver and *kundan* (expensive stone, essential if you want to look like old Rajput nobility). Rajasthani *jootis* – leather slip-ons, either decorated or plain – pinch cruelly when you begin to wear them and often need to be soaked in oil to fit your feet. Once they are 'broken in' though, they are very comfortable.

The **Crafts Museum** and **Cottage Industries Emporium** in Delhi are good places to see the crafts of north India, from teak furniture, wood, marble and papier-mâché objects to lampshades and lamps, *dhurries*, carpets and fabric. Mughal and Rajput **miniature paintings** are beautiful, renowned for their subtle use of colour and delicate lines.

Culture

The culture of India at this time is in a state of enormous flux, with influences from the West being absorbed and resisted at the same time. Indians are looking at their traditional culture and examining it in the light of the new, but the power of the old achievements in *kathak* and *bharatanatyam* (**classical Indian dance**), Urdu **poetry**, Hindi **literature**, traditional vocals and instruments continues and is still very much alive, even though, some classical exponents have been criticized for 'going popular'. The number of Indians writing English literature continues to grow. The trend of dynamic artistic writing in English which began with **Salman Rushdie**'s *Midnight's Children* was taken forward by writers like Amitav Ghosh and Vikram Seth. After **Arundhati Roy's** *The God of Small Things* won the Booker Prize in 1997, a host of other younger writers like Pankaj Mishra, Raj Kamal Jha, Kiran Desai and Jayshree Mishra emerged. Increasingly, the literature and music of the south and northeast of the country are being revived and Delhi is a lively cultural centre that often holds shows, exhibitions and book readings. 'Bollywood', the largest film industry in the world, pumps out its melodramatic song-and-dance performances and some smash box office hits. Younger film-makers are beginning to explore themes like the Mumbai underworld and political corruption.

Home-grown television soaps, new cable channels that show Baywatch and Ally McBeal, and 24-hour news bulletins, as well as lively Internet sites and the fact that an increasing number of Indians are going abroad for education and jobs, places India at a fascinating stage in its history.

Opposite: *A beautifully adorned Rajastani woman.*
Below: *A cinema.*

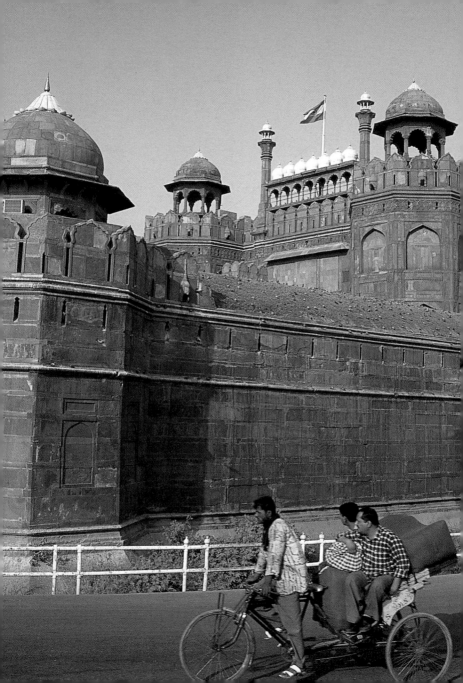

2
Delhi

At first glance, Delhi is overwhelming. The contrasts that abound on its streets today are as extreme and fascinating as its violent but glorious history. Delhi is an unparalleled experience – Connaught Place and its cacophonous traffic jumble of rickshaws, jeeps, street vendors and pedestrians; Old Delhi's narrow lanes with their entangled telephone wires, strong aromas wafting up from boiling pots, goats and drooling cows; ragged beggars at traffic lights and the slums around the railway station where life goes on with a vitality and dignity that is incomprehensible to the outsider; New Delhi with its elegant mansions, luxury hotels, top restaurants and chic shopping emporia – however you choose to spend your time in this city, the experience is bound to remain deeply etched in your memory.

THE SEVEN CITIES OF DELHI

'Delhi has many gates of entry but none for departure' This local saying is validated by the dramatic history of this ancient city. Century after century, Delhi has risen from the ashes of invasions and massacres to blossom again in renewed beauty and glory, and become the multi-layered, vast metropolis that it is today. Depending on your personal preference and schedule, it is possible to spend time in the capital simply soaking up the beguiling atmosphere and enjoying the sights and sounds of a complex culture – there is always something happening on the streets, there is much to taste, hear and see. Alternatively, you can choose to dig deeper through layers

DON'T MISS

*** **Janpath market:** see a range of Rajasthani fabrics, Tibetan crafts and antiques.
*** **The Red Fort:** explore this huge Mughal fort.
*** **Jama Masjid:** climb to the top of the mosque for a good view over Old Delhi.
*** **Chandni Chowk:** take a stroll or rickshaw ride around the narrow, cluttered lanes.
*** **Nizamuddin village:** visit the shrine, and try a Mughal dinner at Dastarkhwan-e-Karim.
*** **Hauz Khas:** stroll along the boutique-lined streets.

Opposite: *Rickshaw at the walls of the Red Fort.*

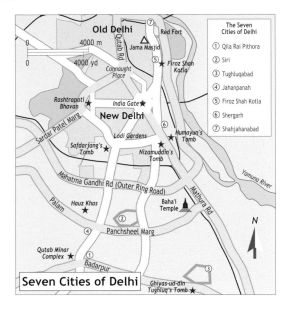

The Seven Cities of Delhi

① Qila Rai Pithora
② Siri
③ Tughluqabad
④ Jahanpanah
⑤ Firoz Shah Kotla
⑥ Shergarh
⑦ Shahjahanabad

Seven Cities of Delhi

of ruined glory and embark on a rewarding discovery journey through the remnants of a powerful and ever-growing empire, testimony to the extravagant dreams of individual rulers and the reversals of fortune. You will discover that there isn't simply **Old Delhi** and **New Delhi**, but that Delhi consists of no fewer than **seven cities**, the ruins of which (over 20,000 sites in total) lie in the middle of the residential districts known as colonies. If it weren't for the frantic urban expansion that has organically merged with ancient debris, many parts of Delhi would be cordoned off as national heritage sites.

The first settlement in the Delhi area is believed to have been **Indraprastha**, which existed between 1000BC and the fourth century AD and appears in the *Mahabharata* as the beautiful capital built by the Pandava brothers, heroes of the epic. There are no traces of this legendary city today, but the site is marked by the Old Fort or Purana Qila, built by the Afghan king Sher Shah in the 16th century. In the eighth century AD the Tomar Rajputs founded Lal Kot. Four centuries later it was overtaken by another Rajput dynasty – the Chauhans – and became **Qila Rai Pithora**, first city of Delhi, found today in the southern suburb of Mehrauli. There is not much left of the first city as the stones of its many Hindu and Jain temples were used in the construction of the Great Mosque in the **Qutab Minar Complex** nearby to the west. The Rajputs were defeated by invading Afghani troops led by Mohammed Ghuri. This ruler's days were numbered, but his Indian provinces remained under the rule of his Turkish general and ex-slave, **Qutab-ud-din-Aibak**, who founded the enduring Delhi **Sultanate**, beginning with the Slave Dynasty, that marked the advent of Islamic rule over Northern India. He also began the construction of an ambitious project, India's first mosque. **Qutab Minar**, at 73m (238 feet) possibly the highest minaret in the world at the time, proclaimed the supremacy of Islam.

In the late 13th century the Khalji clan of Turks took over from the slave sultans and built the second city of Delhi, **Siri**. The most notable feature of this prosperous city remaining today is the *hauz* or water reservoir, which the Sultan built for the citizens – hence the name of the nearby modern complex of **Hauz Khas**, where some of Delhi's best designer boutiques are found. With the advent of the Tughluq sultans in early 14th century, **Tughluqabad**, the third city of Delhi, came into existence, but was abandoned after only five years due to drought. Mad Sultan Mohammed Tughluq migrated his unwilling citizens 15,000km (9321 miles) to the south of Delhi, but returned a few years later to build **Jahanpanah**, Delhi's fourth city, between Qila Rai Pithora and Siri. The next sultan, Feroz Shah, created **Firoz Shah Kotla**, the fifth city, on the banks of the Yamuna River. Following a terrible

Below: *Hauz Khas, once a 13th-century water reservoir.*

sacking of Delhi by the lame Mongol Taimur who slaughtered 50,000 of its residents, the **Lodi** dynasty ruled with an ever-tightening grip, until a rebellion led by **Babur**, a descendant of Genghis Khan, opened a major chapter in Indian history. The capable Babur became the first **Mughal** ruler. His learned son Humayun was driven out by an Afghan king Sher Shah, who managed to build Purana Qila on the Yamuna – known as **Shergarh** (the sixth city), before Humayun returned and reclaimed his throne. What is today known as Old Delhi is in fact the seventh city, named **Shahjahanabad** after the great emperor Shah Jahan (ruler of the universe) who also built the **Taj Mahal**. His rule was interrupted by his greedy sons of whom the most cunning and also the most unpleasant was Aurangzeb, the next emperor.

Another catastrophic plunder of Delhi occurred in the 18th century when the Persian emperor Nadir Shah invaded India. With the appropriation of Shah Jahan's magnificent Peacock Throne, Nadir Shah signaled the decline of the great Mughal era.

Right: *New Delhi, the President's Palace seen through the gates.*

The Mughals survived until the bloody mutiny of 1857 when **Bahadur Shah**, the last emperor, was exiled by the British. By then the capital had been shifted to Calcutta, but during his visit to India in 1911, King **George V** of England announced, to everyone's surprise, that the capital was to be moved back. This was to become New Delhi.

NEW DELHI

With its wide, tree-lined avenues, palatial buildings, foreign embassies, gardens and tidy markets, New Delhi is visitor-friendly and a good place to start your journey. In 1913, noted

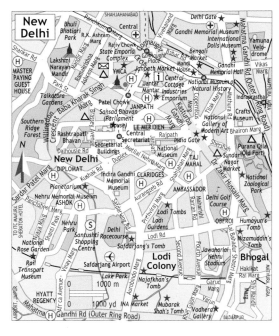

British architect **Edwin Lutyens** was selected to design the new imperial Delhi. He travelled around North India for inspiration but was impressed by little more than the magical Datia Palace (see page 119) and the Buddhist sculptures of Sanchi which also appear in the domes of the **Rashtrapati Bhavan**. After surveying Delhi from elephant-back, Lutyens and his aides decided to build a city 'as an Englishman dressed for the climate'. They proceeded to create an imperial design based on Western classicism, with heterogeneous Indian motifs thrown in, resulting in an imaginative and monumental concoction of styles aspiring to proclaim the supremacy of the British Empire. Lord Hardinge arrived from Calcutta to inaugurate the start of the constructions with a procession along Chandni Chowk where he was injured by a bomb. This added to the various superstitions concerning Delhi.

The cost of the project was extravagant and controversy raged. Thirty thousand labourers were employed, and a

GURGAON

Across the state border in Haryana, Gurgaon is rapidly becoming the eighth city of Delhi. In the last few years, this vast building site has turned from a small town to a city of over 1 million, its enormous apartment blocks acting as commuter dormitories for Delhi yuppies. It also has many multinational offices and some of the area's best shopping malls and restaurants.

Right: *India Gate, World War I memorial.*

railway was built especially for the transportation of building material from the south. By the time it was completed, 500 million tons of material had been carried. Popular leaders Mahatma Gandhi and Nehru commented that such 'vulgar ostentation' was 'in conflict with the best interests of the nation.' But when Lutyens's Delhi was finished, 20 years later, a British historian exclaimed 'I can't describe to you how beautiful it is.'

Rajpath

Rajpath (Kingsway at the time) is the main axle of Lutyens's capital. At its east end stands the imposing cream-sandstone **India Gate**, Delhi's Arc de Triomphe, an all-India war memorial commemorating the 90,000 Indian soldiers who lost their lives fighting for England in World War I. The names of more than 13,000 Indian and British soldiers killed on the northwest frontier and in the Afghan War of 1919 are inscribed on the arch. An eternal flame burns beneath it for those who died in the Indo-Pakistan War of 1971. Just beyond India Gate is the **Canopy**, the last imperial monument, which housed an imposing statue of George V but is now empty after the statue was exiled to the northern ridge of the city. Looking down on Rajpath from India Gate and past the plaza of **Vijay Chowk**, you will see Lutyens's grand achievement – **Rashtrapati Bhavan** with the two **Secretariat Buildings** on each side in perfect symmetry. Built originally as the viceroy's house, Rashtrapati Bhavan is now the official residence of the President of India. Larger than Versailles and containing 340 rooms, this cream and red sandstone edifice with its domes and colonnades is a unique blend of East and West, reminiscent of Mughal tomb, Rajput fortress and colonial palace. In the middle of the court in front of the palace is the **Jaipur Column** built with money donated by the Maharaja of Jaipur. A symbol of victory, the 44m-high (144 feet) column is carved with oak leaves and ends in a bronze lotus from which bursts a crystal star. The Secretariat Buildings, similar in style and grandeur to the Rashtrapati Bhavan, today house the ministries of Foreign Affairs and Finance. In their courtyards are four dominion columns representing Australia, Canada, New Zealand and South Africa, each topped with a globe and a ship.

Behind Rashtrapati Bhavan are the beautiful terraced **Mughal Gardens**, open to the public only in February, following Republic Day. Recreating the Mughal quadrant pattern cut by water channels, it has a butterfly garden around a pool, planted with flowers. Today the park employs 150 gardeners, while at the time of its construction 50 staff were employed solely to scare off birds!

To the north of Rajpath and the Secretariat stands Parliament House, **Sansad Bhavan**. With a red sandstone foundation, cream sandstone middle section and a top storey in plaster (as funds were running short!), this monumental circular construction has

Below: *The South Block of the Secretariat Buildings in New Delhi.*

144 colonnades and three semicircular halls that now house the Council of States, the House of the People and a library. The central circular hall with a 28m (90feet) dome is the place where the Constitution of Independent India was drafted.

Janpath Market ★★★

From Rajpath make your way up along **Janpath**, the north-south artery of Lutyens's Delhi which will take you to **Connaught Place**, the commercial hub of the modern city. Janpath's market is absorbing, so set aside plenty of time for browsing.

Located in a lane off Janpath, it has dazzling authentic Rajasthani textiles sold by a row of hard-bargaining tribal women. If you're prepared to haggle, you won't find the real thing cheaper anywhere else in town. For an orderly, fixed-price selection of the best Indian handicrafts and handlooms – and good service – you can't do better than the two-storeyed **Central Cottage Industries Emporium**, on the corner of Janpath and Tolstoy Marg. If you'd rather browse, the **Tibetan market** has Tibetan jewellery, some real antiques, knick-knacks as well as junk.

Right: *Janpath Market in New Delhi.*

Connaught Place

With its three concentric and seven radial roads that divide it into blocks (from A to N), surrounded by grandiose colonnaded façades, Connaught Place is not just a shopping centre. Named after Duke Connaught, the uncle of King George V, it is a worthy addition to Lutyens's parliamentary city, although another

Above: *The continuous bustle at Connaught Place.*

architect designed it. The first hotels and cinemas of Delhi were built here. Its busy traffic, street vendors, myriad shops catering for all needs and concentration of hotels and restaurants make it a watershed between modern and Old Delhi. It is best explored on foot or by auto rickshaw and ideal for window-shopping, lunches and dinners. Rajiv Chowk Metro station, located under Connaught Place, is the busiest station on Delhi's Metro network. It is also an interchanging point and one can take trains from here to most destinations on the network.

Two interesting markets worth perusing are **Palika Bazaar** (between block G and N), which is underground, so it's cool in summer, and the lively **Bengali Market** (situated on Tansen Marg in central Delhi) where you can taste some of the best Bengali sweets in town at **Nathu's**. Just outside the outer circle, along **Baba Kharak Singh Marg** you will find the **State Emporia Complex** that offers excellent handicrafts from different Indian states. This is the place to buy Kashmiri carpets, shawls and papier-mâché, rather than in the more expensive Kashmir Emporium (in central Delhi). Across the road is a temple to Hanuman, the monkey god. Every Tuesday, a lively market sprawls near the temple where you can find bangles and assorted everyday objects, and have your palms hennaed with traditional designs. To the west of Connaught Place on Mandir Marg, the large, extravagant domes of **Lakshmi**

HOW TO BUILD A DOME

Two more palaces were built by Lutyens: **Hyderabad House** for the prince of Hyderabad (then believed to be the richest man in the world), and **Baroda House** for the Maharaja of Baroda. Like Rashtrapati Bhavan, these palaces have domes built without any support in the following ancient Indian tradition: the labourers stood in a circle, brick in hand, while mortar was laid on and music played. At the sound of a drumbeat, they laid their bricks in perfect harmony, thus instantly creating a ring.

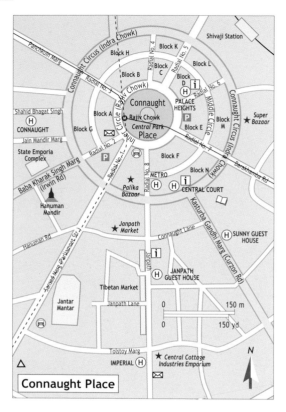

Connaught Place

Narayan Mandir (open daily) are hard to miss. This temple to Lakshmi, the goddess of prosperity, is a good introduction to Hindu temples. Remember to take off your shoes in the reception hall.

Not far from here, in Ashoka Road, is a Sikh temple complex, **Bangla Sahib Gurdwara**, also worth an inspection. Here, beautiful devotional music emanates from the central shrine at all times. Southwest of Connaught Place along Sansad Marg is the surreal pink-and-white **Jantar Mantar**, one of five astrological observatories conceived by Maharaja Jai Singh II – Jaipur's extraordinary ruler in the first half of the 18th century. The sundials can calculate time with astonishing precision. The Jaipur Jantar Mantar is even more impressive and features in the *Guinness Book of Records*. Another place of interest is the **National Rose Garden** (*see* panel on page 44) near the ruins of **Firoz Shah Kotla**. The garden's entrance is Khuni-Darwaza (blood gate – where the British executed two sons of the last emperor), thought to be the surviving gate to **Shergarh**, Sher Shah's city (*see* page 34).

The Museums

New Delhi has a wealth of museums some of which simply must be seen. The **National Museum** (open Tuesday–Sunday, 10:00–17:00) is easily found just south of the Janpath-Rajpath intersection. It is both large in size and in scope and a great way to learn about the permutations of Indian and Asian aesthetics and cultures. Starting with exhibits dating from 5000 years ago, it traces the evolution of art during different dynasties and eras. Highlights are the **Nagaland masks**, the Buddhist gallery, **carpentry** from Gujarat, the display of 300 musical instruments, the **Central Asian** antiquities and the Indian **miniature gallery** (the largest in the world). Suitably housed in the former Jaipur House, built by Lutyens for the Maharaja of Jaipur, the **National Gallery of Modern Art** (open daily 10:00–17:00) offers a retrospective view of Indian art over the last 150 years, including work by poet and artist Rabindranath Tagore, the enigmatic folk art inspired Jamini Roy, Ravi Varma's iconic portraits, and temporary exhibitions by new artists. The popular **Indira Gandhi Memorial Museum** in Safdarjang Road is the tasteful former home of the Gandhi family and contains letters, photos and possessions, including Indira Gandhi's bloodstained sari; part of it is dedicated to her son Rajiv – the clothes he wore when he was assassinated are on display too. The **Nehru Museum** (Teen Murti Marg) up the road is worth a quick look if you are interested in modern Indian history. If, however, you have to choose one museum, that would have to be the **Crafts Museum** (open daily 10:00–17:00) across from the **Purana Qila** (*see* page 50). Here you will find reconstructions of tribal life in different

THE BELGIAN EMBASSY

One of the most remarkable modern buildings in Delhi, the Belgian embassy is tucked away at the southern end of Shanti Path in the diplomatic enclave of Chanakyapuri. Designed by the world-renowned artist Satish Gujral in the early 1980s, it is a unique and highly conceptual blend of modernized traditional Indian forms, such as the cosmic Hindu configuration of the mandala – the architectural concept of dividing the perfect square into further sequential squares – and it echoes, on a larger scale, Gujral's sculptures.

Left: *The National Gallery of Modern Art.*

THE GREAT BUILDERS

Every new ruler of Hindustan had the ambition to create something bigger and better than his predecessors, which is why Delhi is such an astonishingly multi-layered graveyard of dynasties. Every ruler with a vision left his – and occasionally her – mark. Iltutmish, from the Slave Dynasty, built the Qutab Minar Complex, and Ala-ud-din Khalji from the Khalji Dynasty added the beautiful Alai Darwaza or gatehouse to the mosque in the complex, as well as building his own city, Siri. On a larger scale, Giyas-ud-din Tughluq aspired to create a city that was also a defensive outpost, while his son Mohammed, not content with his father's achievement, erected his own city, Jahanpanah (refuge of the world). The Lodi sultans left extravagant tombs, found in Delhi's Lodi Gardens. The Mughals of course took this trend to yet greater heights, the most striking examples being the extravagant and short-lived Fatehpur Sikri (city of victory) near Agra, Agra Fort and the Red Fort in Delhi. It was not enough to be functional – every new architectural project had to be superlative. The Taj Mahal was built to be the most beautiful tomb in the world and, alongside other Mughal architecture, is a vivid illustration of the Mughals' idealistic concept of creating a 'paradise on earth'.

states of India, set in a village complex complete with an entire wooden *haveli* – a traditional mansion with an interior courtyard (*see* page 43). Master weavers work with beautiful textiles and complex patterns, and there are regular dance, music and puppetry performances, and craft displays and sales.

OLD DELHI

There are many old Delhis, but of all of them, the name refers particularly to the walled city of Shah Jahan, Ruler of the World. The fifth great Mughal emperor was a lover of beautiful architecture. When the construction of the Taj Mahal was underway he turned his attention to the traditional Mughal capital and graced it with a grand new city (Shahjahanabad) and, in 1648, with his royal Peacock Throne. Today almost nothing remains of the city walls and only four of its 14 gates survive – **Kashmiri Gate**, the northern entrance to the walled city, and **Delhi Gate** to the south, followed by **Turkman** and **Ajmeri Gates** to the west. The **Red Fort,** from where the emperor governed Hindustan, is still the architectural highlight of the walled city, together with the biggest mosque in India – **Jama Masjid** (Friday Mosque) – also built by Shah Jahan. Pockets of the past glory of Shahjahanabad can be spotted here and there among the colourful decay and chaotic but good-natured human and motor traffic of the main

thoroughfare **Chandni Chowk** (Moonlight Square). Patience and a spirit of adventure are needed to enjoy this most fascinating and enduring part of Delhi. The hard bargaining at sprawling spice and jewellery markets, the leisurely savouring of Mughal meat dishes at **Karim's** restaurant, the seemingly unchanged medieval back streets of Chandni Chowk where goats and children play in the gutters, the stately, beautifully painted *havelis* tucked away behind arches – all this makes for an unforgettable experience of the immortal capital.

Red Fort ★★★

Known as Lal Qila (Red fort) and twice the size of the Agra fort, this mighty palace was Shah Jahan's dream of building 'delightful edifices through which streams of water should flow and the terraces of which should overlook the river'. Though badly damaged in the numerous sackings of Delhi, especially by the British in 1858 when the last emperor was deposed, the fort retains some of its beauty and grandeur. The entrance is through **Lahori Gate** outside which a congregation of rickshaws and vendors accost potential customers. You may be offered the services of a guide. It is better to look for one inside the walls if you don't already have one. Alternatively you may prefer to

> #### THE MARKETS OF OLD DELHI
>
> **Chawri Bazaar:** located west of Jama Masjid, sells masks, lamps, ashtrays, brass and copper statuettes of Hindu gods.
> **Dariba Kalan:** explore the jewellers' street.
> **Kinari Bazaar:** sells fine wedding and festival apparel
> **Nai Sarak:** this street running from Chawri Bazaar to Chandni Chowk specializes in beautiful handmade paper and stationery.
> **Sadar Bazaar:** past the Fatehpuri Masjid, a wholesale spice market selling the best spices and nuts in Delhi.

Above: *The 60-pillared Diwan-i-Am, or Hall of Public Audience.*

ROSES

The rose was a favourite Mughal flower. Shan Jahan's favourite sweet was rose-flavoured *gulab jamun*. Nur Jahan (Light of the World), the beloved wife of Emperor Jahangir, who was known to ride into battle with him and who built her father the splendid tomb of Itimad-ud-Daulah in Agra, bathed in rose petals. She is thus reputed to have discovered *gulab attar* or rose perfume. Her imposing bath, given to her by Jahangir on their wedding, is in Akbar Mahal in Agra Fort. The **Rose Gardens** near the ruins of Feroz Shah Kotla are lovely in February and March.

enjoy this sight at your own leisure. Inside the walls, you will stroll along Chatta Chowk, a bazaar lane that used to service the courtiers with silver, jewels and brocades, and which today offers little more than predictable souvenirs – with the occasional gem. At the beginning of the lane, on the left-hand side and up a staircase, there is a jewellery shop selling interesting if somewhat overpriced silver. The official gateway is **Naqqar-Khana** (drum house) where thunderous music was played to announce the arrival of the emperor. Through the gateway is the red sandstone Hall of Public Audience, **Diwan-i-Am**, where the emperor sat on a raised marble throne to receive his visitors, high and low, and discuss public matters. Executioners stood by, ready to carry out the emperor's sentences. The audience ended with a review of the royal elephants and horses. The pavilion is decorated with *pietra dura* carvings of flowers, birds and a surprising scene of Orpheus with a lute, designed by a Frenchman. The private palaces are beyond the Diwan-i-Am, parallel to the now retreating river. To the far left lie two marble pavilions, the only remains of what used to be the regal, lamp-lit, richly decorated gardens of **Hayat Baksh Bagh** (life-giving gardens). The first significant building to the east is the ethereal **Moti Masjid** or Pearl Mosque, built by Shah Jahan's pious son and usurper of power Aurangzeb for his private prayers. Behind the mosque are the lavishly carved and miraculously preserved marble royal baths or *hammam*. The next building along the marble pavilion of **Diwan-i-Khas**, or Hall of Private Audience, is the political heart of the complex and aesthetically the most beautiful construction. In the centre of the bejewelled and decorated pavilion stands the Peacock Throne, pride of the emperor, entirely made of gold and inlaid with a wealth of precious stones. It was taken as loot by the Persian Nadir Shah in his bloody sacking of the capital in the 18th century. At this throne, the emperor received important visitors and reflected on matters of state. One of the arches bears an inscription composed by the famous poet Amir Khusrau: 'If on earth there be a place of bliss, it is this, it is this, it is this'.

The **Khas Mahal** was the emperor's private quarters, with separate apartments for prayer, eating and sleeping. He made public appearances twice a day on his octagonal balcony before a gathering of citizens down on the banks of the river. One of the rooms has an exquisite *jaali* (marble screen) representing the scales of justice.

Conveniently close by is the **Rang Mahal** or Painted Palace which housed the royal harem. The emperor would retire here for his lunch to discuss housekeeping matters with his favourite daughter Jahanara, first lady since the death of his wife, Mumtaz Mahal. The Palace had a silver ceiling which has since been defaced, and a lotus-shaped

ARTS AND CRAFTS

In Sanskrit the word *shilpi* means both artist and craftsman. In India there is no traditional distinction between crafts and arts and this can be appreciated at the Crafts Museum near the Purana Qila. Here, over 20,000 showcases of the best in tribal art are on display. You can watch the craftsmen in action and purchase their work. The master weaver at the museum creates intricately embroidered saris which remain as museum exhibits – they are truly works of art and can take up to eight months to make. There is also live music and tribal dancing in the open courtyard.

Left: *Red Fort, latticed screen in the Khas Mahal.*

marble pool with a silver fountain. The last palace, **Mumtaz Mahal**, is obscure in origin – though it most likely housed some of the harem – and now contains the palace museum. It is worth a quick look.

Jama Masjid (Friday Mosque) ★★★

The last of Shah Jahan's great projects was completed two years before he lost his throne to his son Aurangzeb. The Jama Masjid is the largest mosque in India, one of the largest of Islam and it cost one million rupees to build. It is at the heart of Muslim life in Old Delhi, the equivalent of the Nizamuddin village in South Delhi and a spiritual counterpoint to the Red Fort. Its striped minarets and three onion domes dominate Old Delhi and are worth the climb for a breathless panorama of the city. The vast open courtyard with a water tank in the middle for washing before prayer, accommodates up to 20,000 worshippers, though on most days prayers take place inside the main prayer hall to the west (facing Mecca). Note the striking black marble inlay in the decorations inside and on the domes. The vast sandstone steps leading up to the mosque from three sides are a social hub. Here worshippers read the

Left: *Chandni Chowk, Old Delhi's main arterial road.*
Opposite: *Muslim heart of the Old City – Jama Masjid (Friday Mosque).*

THE TWO KARIMS

The original Karim is in Matia Mahal, a lane south of the Jama Masjid, the other at the heart of Nizamuddin village. The two restaurants are run by the successors of the original owners who were chefs at the Mughal court. The idea was to bring royal cuisine to the people. The one in Matia Mahal has five dining halls and offers great hands-on displays of Muslim cooking in the internal courtyard: brews in huge pots and various methods of making *roti* and *naan*. There is a variety of excellent kebabs and very good vegetarian dishes. The family recipes are a secret not revealed even to the staff in the kitchen: the women in the family make the elaborate spice mixture themselves, as well as Karim's special *khir* (rice and milk pudding in earthenware). A favourite is the *badam pasanda*, almond and curd lamb. No alcohol is available.
Karim's, Jama Masjid, Gali Kababian, Old Delhi 110006, tel: (011) 2326 9880 or 2326 4981.
Karim's, 168/2, Hzt. Niza-Muddin West, New Delhi 110016, tel: (011) 2435 5458 or 2435 8300, e-mail: khpl@del3.vsnl.net.in
There is a third Karim's (Mughal Palace) in Noida.

Qur'an and gossiping men and vendors sell sweet meats and kebabs. You will need to remove your shoes and cover your legs and arms before entering the mosque. Opposite the south entrance is **Karim's restaurant**, a compulsory detour (*see* right panel).

Chandni Chowk ★★★

You can make your way to the main thoroughfare of Old Delhi either from the **Red Fort**, which is at its eastern end, or from the **Jama Masjid** through the labyrinthine side streets around **Dariba Kalan**. In either case, taking a cycle rickshaw is a more stress-free alternative to walking, which for the first-time visitor, can be overwhelming. Chandni Chowk (Moonlight Square) was constructed by Jahanara, Shah Jahan's favourite daughter. Originally, there was an octagonal pool in front of the Lahori Gate of the Red Fort, into which a branch of the Stream of Paradise – a watering system in the palace – flowed creating a beautiful effect in the moonlight and giving the avenue its name. It was lined with trees and water channels among which the liveliest commerce in the East took place. If your starting point is the Red Fort, the first sight of interest, straight to your left, is the **Jain Temple**,

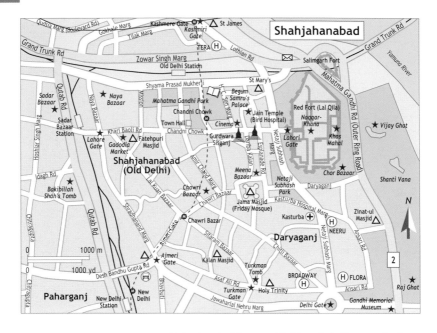

which also doubles as a **bird hospital**. The temple dates from the 16th century and has some gilded ornamentation and carvings. In its courtyard is the bird hospital, housing sick birds in tune with the Jain principle of preserving all life. Regular patients here are partridges wounded in the partridge fights that are among Old Delhi-*wallahs*' (residents) favourite pastimes. Further down Chandni Chowk is the large **Gurdwara Sisganj**, a Sikh temple dedicated to a guru beheaded by Emperor Aurangzeb. Here, he also displayed the beheaded corpse of his learned and liberal brother Dara Shukoh, favourite son of Shah Jahan.

Just around the corner from the Gurdwara is **Dariba Kalan** the jewellers' street, where you can find exceptional new and antique silverware at low prices. To the left is **Kinari Bazaar**, a glittering market lane selling wedding and festival apparel including saris, masks of Hindu deities and swords. Every object here shines with gold or silver tinsel. At the corner of Dariba Kalan and Chandni Chowk you can make a quick stop at the popular sweet shop of Naim

Opposite: *Site of Mahatma Gandhi's cremation, now a public park.*

Chand Jain, selling *jalebi* twirls (fried treacle tubes soaked in hot syrup), similar in sweetness to *gulab jamun*. Further down and across Chandni Chowk is the British-built **Town Hall** (1860s) behind which lies the peaceful **Mahatma Gandhi Park**, once built as the Queen's Gardens and today a favourite haunt for *sadhus* (Hindu ascetics). Towards the west end of the avenue is **Fatehpuri Mosque**, financed by Begum Fatehpuri, one of Shah Jahan's wives. Outside the mosque begin stalls selling nuts and dried fruit which gradually blend into spice stalls – a sign that the intense **spice market** or **Sadar Bazaar** is approaching. It is tucked away behind a gateway, so ask for directions. You will find every imaginable spice here, if you have the nerve to sneeze your way through the noisy throngs!

Memorial Ghats

Wherever there is a river in India, there are *ghats* or river steps – for washing, fetching water, bathing, and executing cremations. Along the bank of the Yamuna, right of Mahatma Gandhi Road, there are several *ghats* that are also memorials to Indian politicians. **Raj Ghat** at the south end is where Mahatma Gandhi was cremated in 1948. There is now a moving memorial on the spot. Nearby is the **Gandhi Memorial Museum**, celebrating the

life and ideas of the Mahatma. Further up the river is **Shanti Vana** (Forest of Peace) where the first prime minister of India, Jawaharlal Nehru, as well as his daughter Indira Gandhi and her two sons Sanjay and Rajiv were cremated. **Vijay Ghat** is dedicated to India's second prime minister, Lal Bahadur Shastri.

SOUTH DELHI

South of Lutyens's Delhi is where you will find traces of some of the **old cities** merging with fashionable complexes like **Hauz Khas**, and the fascinating medieval Muslim enclave of **Nizamuddin**.

Purana Qila and Sundar Nagar

East of India Gate and between Mathura and Outer Ring Road lie the splendid ruins of Purana Qila – today the scene of theatrical and musical performances. At this multi-layered site, centuries of dreams and fates of different rulers overlap. The earliest traces here are from the legendary city of **Indraprastha**, which features in the *Mahabharata*. But what still stands today are the remnants of **Shergarh**, the sixth city of Delhi built by the Afghan ruler Sher Shah. Having moved from Agra to Delhi, the Mughal emperor Humayun dreamt of ruling from his new city **Dinpanah** (Shelter of Faith) when Sher Shah invaded and forced him into exile. He expanded the city of Humayun northwards and called it Shergarh. The entrance gate stands by Firoz Shah Kotla and two of the principal buildings of Purana Qila survive: Qal'a-i-Kuhna-Masjid (Old Fort Mosque) consisting of five arches made of marble-inlaid sandstone, and Sher Mandal where Huma-

Below: *The Old Fort, Purana Qila, built by the Afghan Sher Shah.*

yun fell to his death (*see* right panel). You can ascend the stairs on which he stumbled, and enjoy a panoramic view of Delhi and the Yamuna River. Making your way south to **Humayun's Tomb**, you will pass through **Sundar Nagar** market where a number of excellent shops sell antique jewellery and art for the connoisseur.

Above: *Humayun's Tomb, the predecessor of the Taj Mahal.*

Humayun's Tomb

Although Emperor Humayun spent 15 years in exile while Sher Shah occupied Delhi, his reign marks the beginning of the Mughal golden era. A learned and refined man, he died in a fall from the top of his library after he had returned to reclaim the seat of power. His wife Bega (Haji) Begum undertook the construction of a splendid tomb which became a landmark in an epoch of great Mughal architecture, reaching its apogee in the **Taj Mahal**. Its Persian architect used the Qur'anic concept of Paradise in a garden setting. The quadrangle divisions of its grounds, introducing the *charbagh* (four-garden) idea, is seen on a larger scale in the Taj Mahal. Mughals entombed here are Dara Shukoh (favourite son of Shah Jahan, who was murdered by his brother Aurangzeb), emperors Farrukhsiyar and Alamgir – both murdered, and Bega Begum, the tomb's creator. Open daily.

HUMAYUN'S DEATH

Emperor Humayun was exiled to Persia after Afghan Emperor Sher Shah invaded Delhi and created the city of **Shergarh** at the site of ancient city **Purana Qila**. Only two of the fort buildings survive today, including the octagonal Sher Mandal which Humayun, on his return to Delhi, made into his library. It was here, at the top of the stairs, that he stood one night looking out for the transit of Venus, tripped over his robes and plummeted to his death. His tomb, the first great Mughal tomb, was built by his widow Bega Begum who is also buried there.

Lodi Gardens

Named after the Lodi Sultan dynasty which ruled Delhi from the mid-15th century to the 1520s, the garden grounds today contain several tombs of Lodi and Sayyid sultans (the dynasty before the Lodis). Best to visit at dusk when the tombs are lit up and the park is quietly overrun with joggers.

Safdarjang's Tomb

In contrast to Humayun's mausoleum, this tomb was built in the last throes of Mughal power and marks the end of this golden age. Safdarjang was an influential and progressive minister to the Emperor Ahmad Shah in the mid-18th century. The emperor himself, described as 'a vicious, dissipated, perfidious, pusillanimous and utterly worthless young man', was eventually duly deposed. Safdarjang's son spent 300,000 rupees on his father's tomb, marking the last and decadent phase of Mughal architecture. The rooftop views are worth a climb.

Nizamuddin ★★★

Nizamuddin, named after a 13th-century Muslim prophet, is a prosperous residential area at whose heart lies a village dating from medieval times. It is accessible from the south via **Mathura Road**. Stroll along its busy, narrow lanes passing through great wooden gates, and savour the Muslim way of life with its kebab aromas and the distant sound of Sufi religious chanting or qawwali. For women, it is imperative to cover legs, arms and heads, especially as you near the *dargah* or shrine of the saint. Entering the shrine area, you pass stalls selling rose petals, Islamic books, CDs of *qawwali*, incense and other indispensables

---

QAWWALI

Qawwali is a devotional music form practised by the Sufi Muslims of India and Pakistan. Today's *qawwals* (exclusively male singers) claim descent from the poet Amir Khusrau, during whose anniversary the singing goes on day and night. The chief mystic associated with this music is Hizrat Nizamuddin and *qawwali* can be heard most reliably in his shrine in Nizamuddin village, especially at festival times. The chanting, accompanied by *tabla* (hand drums) and harmonium, is incantatory and known to induce hypnotic states, associated with spiritual ecstasy in listeners. Despite its religious nature, *qawwali* is also hugely popular and some of its top performers have recorded CDs and achieved star status.

for the visit to Nizamuddin's tomb. Before entering the shrine complex you must leave your shoes with a shoe keeper who will give you a token in exchange for a few rupees. You could be approached by smart men asking you to 'sign the book', i.e. give a donation.

The ascetic Hazrat Nizamuddin lived here for 90 years and had a large following. Belonging to the Chishti order of Sufis, he believed that spiritual ecstasy could be reached through music. To this day, some 200 families related to Nizamuddin and his disciples live from donations to the shrine. Surrounding Nizamuddin's shrine are the smaller tombs of some of his noted disciples: the poet Amir Khusrau, whose poetry set to music is still heard here, especially during the celebration of his anniversary in April when the *qawwali* continues throughout the night, as well as the mighty Mughal emperor Muhammed Shah and Jahanara, Shah Jahan's favourite daughter whose tomb is filled with earth, in accordance with her wish to have nothing but grass cover her grave. A large sandstone mosque to the left, the oldest building in the area, dates from 1325 and is actively in use at least five times a day. You may exit through the northern gate on the other side of the tomb, where you will find a stepwell with holy water, built by Ghiyasuddin Tughlaq (who also built the **Tughluqabad Fort**).

Opposite: *The imposing Bara Gumbaz Tomb located in Lodi Gardens.* **Below** *Nizamuddin's Tomb at the heart of Nizamuddin Village.*

Hauz Khas ★★★

Midway between Safdarjang and the Qutab Minar, Hauz Khas village is a cluster of elegant designer boutiques, antique shops and restaurants flanked by the remains of Delhi's second city Siri and a deer park. The

pleasant relaxed atmosphere of the shopping lanes leads you into shops stocked with a variety of Indian crafts and designs – from furniture and lampshades to high quality jewellery and clothing. There are also some galleries where you can purchase contemporary Indian art. Upon reaching the end of the main street you will come face to face with the remains of the great water reservoir or *hauz* and its adjacent ruins of a university, built at a later stage by Firoz Shah, as well as a number of tombs that include the humble one of Firoz Shah himself. The ancient grounds are popular with picnickers. At night the ruins are lit up and a number of stylish rooftop restaurants in the village complex offer a magical view and good food.

Baha'i Temple

Shaped like a giant lotus flower and made from white Rajasthani marble, the Baha'i Temple dominates the Kalkaji area in the southeast of the city. It is somewhat reminiscent of the Sydney Opera House in its modernist boldness. Its central hall reaches 34m (112 feet). To the south, the contrasting **Kalkaji Temple** – dedicated to the blood-thirsty Hindu goddess Kali – is a testimony to the endurance of tradition and ancient faiths.

THE CURSE OF NIZAMUDDIN

When the first of the Tughluq dynasty of Sultans, Ghiyas-ud-din Tughluq, began the construction of his new city – now the third city of Delhi – he allegedly refused to build a Sufi shrine. Thereupon the Sufi saint Nizamuddin prophesied that the new citadel would remain uninhabited. This curse was fulfilled when the Sultan died in a freak accident and his son, Mohammed, abandoned the city due to a water shortage. Today, Tughluqabad is the most melancholic of Delhi's seven cites. Walking over its ruins, the look over the aggressive new suburban sprawl across the plain is a powerful reminder of the continuous rise and fall of powerful empires.

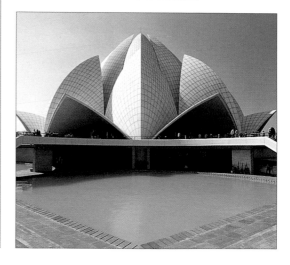

Qutab Minar Complex

In the 8th century, the Tomar Rajput clan built the citadel of **Lal Kot**. Four centuries later another Rajput clan took over and renamed the city **Qila Rai Pithora**, the first city of Delhi. Most of this ancient site was destroyed by the invading Afghan armies who established the **Delhi Sultanate** that marked the beginning of a long Muslim rule over Northern India. Many Hindu temples were destroyed and their intricately carved stones used to build the first Islamic monument of India – **Quwwat-ul-Islam Masjid** (Might of Islam Mosque). The first Muslim ruler, **Qutab-ud-din-Aibak** (see page 10), wasted no time and embarked on the con-

struction of the mosque surrounding an ancient iron pillar. The majestic **Qutab Minar**, a 73m (238 feet) minaret in red sandstone and the most enduring landmark of Delhi, was thought to have been built by Aibak's successor and son-in-law, Iltutmish. It is intricately carved and inscribed with excerpts from the Qur'an. However, recent research shows that all the Medieval Muslims did was put a fancy new coat on a tower built nearly 2000 years previously as a giant sundial.

In the 14th century, Emperor Feroz Shah undertook some repairs of the minaret, adding two storeys in marble and a cupola that was replaced by the British, but later mocked and removed; today it stands on the lawns as a canopy. Unfortunately, access to the inside staircase that

Above: The majestic Qutab Minar, the oldest landmark of Delhi.
Opposite: The lotus-shaped Baha'i Temple.

leads up to the superb balconies has been closed due to suicides and accidents. A gatehouse (**Alai Darwaza**) to the mosque was built by another ruler. This graceful yet solid structure made from red sandstone and white marble has intricate carvings and lotus-bud motifs, all elements which were to reappear in countless Indian buildings in the centuries to come. After touring the complex, an English bishop observed that 'they built like giants, and they finished like jewellers'. Next to the gate, inside the mosque courtyard, stands the mysterious **Iron Pillar**, the single non-Islamic structure in the complex. It bears Sanskrit inscriptions and dates from the 4th century Gupta period. Its origins are unknown, as is the technique used to ensure that the pure iron has remained totally rust-free. Legend has it that whoever manages to encircle the pillar with their arms will have their wish fulfilled. With the pillar now fenced off, the wishes have to wait.

Above: *People used to grasp the Iron Pillar at Qutab Minar Complex in order to make their wishes come true.*

Opposite: *Tughluqabad Fort, once the powerful seat of the first Tughluq Sultan.*

About 1km (0.6 miles) to the west is **Mehrauli village**. The detour is worth making for the boutiques, the good Italian café, and the smattering of ruins and tombs in the area. Most noted is the octagonal tomb of Adham Khan, also known as Bhul-Bhulaiyan (labyrinth) for its intricate passages. This general and foster brother of emperor Akbar was repeatedly thrown from the walls of Agra fort (on the order of the emperor) after murdering the imperial chief minister. His tomb was built at Akbar's order.

Tughluqabad

8km (5 miles) east of Qutab Minar stand the remains of the **third city of Delhi**, built by Ghiyas-ud-din Tughluq, the first of the Tughluq sultans who reigned from the early 14th- to the early 15th century. The city consisted of three parts: the massive fort (near the entrance today) with 13 gates, the palaces to the left of the citadel, and to the north the grid-planned city of which some streets can still be traced. Today, only a tower and some subterranean passages remain, and the ruins are haunted by Rhesus monkeys and nomads. It is believed that when the new citadel was built, the saint Nizamuddin predicted it was soon to be abandoned and inhabited only by Gujjar robbers (*see* page 54). The sultan intended to punish him but met an untimely death. His eccentric son Mohammed took over, but had to leave Tughluqabad only five years after its completion due to a lack of fresh water. He moved 1500km (930 miles) southwards with his people, only to return and found the fourth city of Delhi, **Jahanpanah**, north of the Qutab Minar (not much remains of it today). The impressive mausoleum of Ghyias-ud-din, made from red sandstone and marble, contains the remains of the sultan, his wife and their son.

NEEMRANA FORT PALACE-HOTEL

On the main highway from Delhi to Jaipur, about 120km (76 miles) from Delhi, there is a magical Rajasthani hilltop fort-palace. It was built in the mid-15th century by one Raja Rajdeo, who had fled from the aftermath of the Muslim invasions. An Indian art historian and a Frenchman converted it into a stunningly atmospheric hotel, with great taste and attention to detail. Decorated with hand-printed textiles and antique doors and furniture, this is India's oldest heritage hotel and a worthwhile detour on the way to Jaipur or back to Delhi. On weekends, visitors from Delhi flock here. The hotel also offers a buffet breakfast on the rooftop veranda and fabulous character 'loos with a view'. Tel: (01494) 246006 0068, www.neemranahotels.com

Delhi at a Glance

BEST TIMES TO VISIT

The **coolest** time to visit Delhi is between October and February. **March** and **April** get warm, reaching scorching temperatures in **May** and **June** – often accompanied by dust storms. The **monsoon** season usually starts around **July** and is best avoided because it also brings mosquitoes. **September** is humid and muggy, with temperatures in the 30s, but it can still be pleasant. **October** and **November** are the best months to visit.

GETTING THERE

Indira Gandhi International Airport, tel: (011) 3989 3333 (reservations, check-in, flight information), is a 30-minute drive southwest of the city centre. Book a hotel room at the reservations desk in the departure hall. Taxi rates for airport transfers are normally fixed, with a surcharge at night. There are two main railway stations – **New Delhi Station** and **Delhi Station** in Old Delhi. Railway bookings: **International Tourist Bureau**, New Delhi Railway Station, tel: (011) 2340 5156 or 2334 6804, fax: 2334 3050, e-mail: itbnrind@nda.vsnl.net.in There are flights and trains to both Agra and Jaipur.
Air India, tel: 1800 22 7722, e-mail: call.del@airindia.in
British Airways, tel: (011) 2565 2078; **Virgin Atlantic**, tel: (011) 4130 3030; **Etihad**, tel: (011) 3901 3901; **Indian Airlines**, tel: (011) 2463 1337.

GETTING AROUND

Take a **taxi** for longer distances, including to and from the airport. Negotiate the fare first or use a set-rate taxi from the DTTDC (see page 59). There are taxi stands in Connaught Place and all around New Delhi. In New Delhi **autorickshaws** are a good and cheap alternative to the taxi. As every journey involves haggling, it is worth hiring a taxi or auto-rickshaw by the day. In Old Delhi and for smaller stretches, **cycle-rickshaws** are safe. Delhi now has three **metro** lines. For details, visit www.delhimetrorail.com
Car rental companies in Delhi include State Express, tel: (011) 2685 5483 or 2685 2712 or 2652 4006; Swift Car Rentals, tel: (011) 2696 0202; Bal Tourist Transport Service, tel: (011) 2338 4301 or 2338 8880.

WHERE TO STAY

LUXURY

The Maurya New Delhi, Diplomatic Enclave, tel: (011) 2611 2233; fax: (011) 2611 3333. Three wings, a special floor for women travellers, a pool and health club, shopping centre and some fine restaurants, including Bukhara, specializing in northwest frontier cuisine, and Dum Phukt, imperial cuisine unlike other Indian food.
Imperial, Janpat, tel: (011) 2334 1234 or 4150 1234, fax: (011) 2334 2255; luxury@theimperialindia.com www.theimperialindia.com

Established hotel from the 30s, with authentic Raj ambience and a recent overhaul. Great location, outdoor bar, breakfast buffet and a fine Asian restaurant – the Thai Spice Route.
Taj Mahal, 1 Mansingh Road, tel: (011) 2302 6162, fax: (011) 2302 6070; mahal.delhi@tajhotels.com www.tajhotels.com
Splendid Raj-style ambience, highly ornate. Has one of the best French restaurants in Delhi, Longchamp; an Indian *Mughlai* restaurant, Haveli, with live music; and the exceptional Chinese House of Ming.
Taj Palace Hotel, Sardar Patel Marg, Diplomatic Enclave, tel: (011) 2611 0202; fax: (011) 2611 0808; palace.delhi@tajhotels.com www.tajhotels.com
The ultimate in luxury, just 10 minutes' drive from the airport.
Ambassador, Sujan Singh Park (near India Gate), tel: (011) 2463 2600, fax: (011) 2463 2252; ambassador.delhi @tajhotels.com www.tajhotels.com
Large, comfortable rooms, disco and one of the best South Indian restaurants.

UPMARKET TO MID-RANGE

Claridges, 12 Aurangzeb Road, tel: (011) 2301 0211, fax: (011) 2301 0625; e-mail: info@claridges.com Stylish, with pool and a touch of decadence. Restaurants include Dhaba (Indian), Jade Garden (Chinese) and Pickwick

(Continental). Outdoor restaurant and bar.

Hotel Broadway, 4/15A Asaf Ali Road, tel: (011) 2327 3821. Just west of Delhi Gate, Chor Bizarre – top restaurant of Old Delhi, views over Jama Masjid.

BUDGET

Ahuja Residency, Delhi, 193 Golf Links, tel: (011) 2462 2255; www.ahujaresidency. com Delightful guesthouse in a 50s mansion near Khan Market. Rooms vary in size and style. Book ahead.

Ahuja Residency, Gurgaon, N3/36, DLF City, Phase II Gurgaon, tel: (0124) 401 9335-37, fax: (0124) 401 5403; jaideep@ahujaresidency.com Good corporate accommodation, convenient to the airport.

Master Paying Guest Accommodation, R-500 New Rajinder Nagar, tel: (011) 2874 1089; www.master-guesthouse.com Small (only 4 rooms) guesthouse carefully designed and run along spiritual principles; roof terrace, reiki treatments.

Hotel Palace Heights, D-26/28, Connaught Place, tel: (011) 4358 2610, fax: 4358 2640. Nice but small rooms, some air conditioned. Terrace, Internet café, reasonably priced.

Most of the best restaurants are in the hotels. Check out the stunning Thai Blue Elephant and Baluchi (Northern Indian) at the Hotel InterContinental in Barakhamba Road; the sublime, low-priced South Indian Coconut Grove in Hotel Indraprastha, 19 Ashoka Rd, tel: (011) 2336 8553, and Le Belvedere and Pierre, two fine French restaurants at Le Meridien, Windsor Place, Janpath, tel: (011) 2371 0101. In town, Connaught Place has a wide selection (see panel, page 38).

Dilli Haat, opp. INA Market. tel: (011) 462 9365. The best place to find fresh snacks. Cheap, with great atmosphere.

The Big Chill Café, 68A Khan Market, tel: (011) 4175 7588. Delhi's best loved café; salads, pasta, cakes and ice creams.

Karim's, see panel, page 47.

Pindi, 16 Pandara Road Market, tel: (011) 2338 7932. Pleasant, friendly *dhaba* restaurant, with air-conditioning and affordable north Indian food.

Turquoise Cottage, 81/3 Adchini, Sri Aurobindo Marg, tel: (011) 2685 3896. Smart Thai/Chinese restaurant near the Qutab Minar; dim sum and barbecue, with a trendy bar. Book ahead Wed, Fri, Sat.

Village Bistro Complex, 12 Hauz Khas village, tel: (011) 2685 3857. Top Indian cuisine, outdoor dining with view of South Delhi.

Tours of Delhi are organized through your hotel or the offices below. **Government of India Tourist Office**, 88 Janpath, tel: (011) 2332 0008; www.tourismofindia.com **Delhi Tourism & Transport Development Corporation** (**DTTDC**), 18A D.D.A.SCO Complex, tel: (011) 2464 7005; www.delhitourism.nic.in **Central Reservations Office**, Coffee Home I, Baba Kharak Singh Marg, opp. Hanuman Temple; tel: (011) 2336 3607 or 2336 5358. Counters at the two main railway stations and at the International Airport.

All-India Institute of Medical Sciences, Ansari Nagar, Sri Aurobindo Marg, tel: (011) 2658 8500. Open 24 hours.

Thomas Cook, Connaught Place; tel: (011) 2341 6585.

American Express, Personal Services; tel: (95124) 280 1800 or 98109 00800.

There are many ATM machines and internet cafés, particularly around Connaught Place. *First City, The Delhi City, City Info* and *Star Delhi Online* are all good listings magazines.

DELHI	J	F	M	A	M	J	J	A	S	O	N	D
AVERAGE TEMP. °C	14	17	23	29	34	35	31	30	30	27	21	16
AVERAGE TEMP. °F	57	63	73	84	93	95	88	86	86	81	70	61
HOURS SUN DAILY	11	12	12	12	14	14	14	14	13	12	12	11
RAINFALL mm	25	22	17	7	8	65	211	173	150	31	1	5
RAINFALL in	1	0.9	0.7	0.3	0.3	2.5	8.2	6.8	5.9	1.2	0.04	0.2

3
Jaipur

Jaipur is the capital of **Rajasthan** – one of India's most fascinating, historical and colourful states. This gateway to the vast **Thar Desert** was once the seat of the fierce and independent Rajput rulers; enduring showcase of the rigidity of the caste system; and today a bustling, surreal city of 5.2 million where slums coexist with opulent palaces. This is also the most visited part of India, after Agra. Until independence in 1947 this was a self-contained kingdom known as **Rajputana** or Land of Kings, consisting of as many as 22 states ruled for centuries by the Rajputs or princes. The most remarkable of these were the **Kachhawaha Rajputs**, a warrior clan whose arrival to these parts is traced back to the 12th century. At first denied power due to alleged low birth, they successfully established themselves, claiming descent from the sun and moon. They performed ritual cleansing through fire and lived by a strict and bloody code of honour which was applied not only when dealing with invaders – such as the Muslims – but also among their own families. The Rajputs placed themselves in a caste above all others and proceeded to rule Rajputana with considerable efficiency for the next six centuries from their capital **Amber**. They heroically fought off the onslaughts of the sultans of Delhi. When the Mughals came into power, it was the great emperor **Akbar** who first induced the Rajputs to cooperate with the new rulers by marrying a Kachhawaha princess. This augmented the prosperity of Rajputana and created an unprecedented united Hindustan.

DON'T MISS

*** Hawa Mahal: see the ornate façade of the 'Palace of Winds'.
*** Jaipur City Palace: in the heart of the old city, now part of the Maharajah Sawai Man Singh II Museum.
*** Jantar Mantar Observatory: built by Sawai Jai Singh II in the 18th century.
*** Bazaars: explore the many colourful street stalls.
*** Ram Niwas Gardens: housing the magnificent Albert Hall and an old zoo.

Opposite: *A bright-eyed little girl dressed for a street wedding in Jaipur.*

ONE AND A QUARTER

Jai Singh was crowned ruler of Amber at the age of 12. When he was 15 the Mughal emperor Aurangzeb tried to remove him by sending him to fight against a tribe further south. When he refused, he was brought before the emperor. Aurangzeb enquired how the young king intended to protect his kingdom and life. Jai Singh answered that he expected the emperor himself to protect him, just as a groom would protect his bride. The emperor was so impressed by his wit that he called him *Sawai* (one and a quarter), a title that was passed on to all Kachhawaha rulers from then on. A flag and a quarter of a flag was flown above the palaces of Jaipur as a reminder to other rulers.

In the 18th century, the most talented and visionary of Rajputs, **Jai Singh II**, built the new capital of Jaipur calling it after himself. He had been crowned ruler of Amber at the tender age of 12, after the death of his father. The first three or so decades of his rule were spent consolidating his power through active service to the Mughals and his kingdom, winning substantial military, diplomatic and financial success. Finally, on the laurels of a brilliant career, at the age of 38, he was able to rest and dedicate himself to his favourite pastimes: art and science. With the immense fortune he had amassed, and with the help of gifted Bengali architect **Vidyadhar Bhattacharaya**, he embarked on a grandiose project, the first of its kind in northern India – building a city from scratch.

THE PINK CITY

Jaipur has remained virtually unchanged from its original plan. It is as vibrant and commercially alive now as it was in the time of Jai Singh II. The construction took only seven years, by which time a glorious **City Palace** was built, as well as temples, markets, *havelis* (town-houses for the aristocracy), residential districts and the extraordinary **Jantar Mantar** is the largest stone observatory in the world – all still in place today. The fantastic **Hawa Mahal** or Palace of Winds was built later that century by another maharaja for his harem. The characteristic **pink** colour of the buildings was a later addition: it was applied to the central district in 1856 as a gesture of welcome on the occasion of the visit of British Prince Albert and it has remained so ever since. Municipal regulations require each homeowner to repaint their façade regularly in order to maintain the appealing pink look of the city. Although many sights of interest are within the Pink City, modern Jaipur comprises more than Jai Singh's walled city. Palaces are scattered all around, as are slums – one third of the population live without sewage. The combination of **pollution** and **heat** in the summer is unbearable, so try

Opposite: *View of the Pink City from the breathtaking Hawa Mahal, or Palace of Winds.*

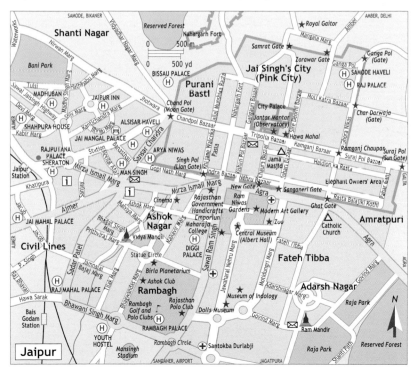

MANDALA

The sacred Hindu scriptures, the *Vedas*, conceived the concept of a Cosmic Man whose body could be seen as an abstract numerical system on the basis of which the material world could be constructed. The buildings in Jaipur are designed to reflect this principle. The *Vasta Purusha Mandala* is a mathematical concept based on the *Vedas*, where the *mandala* is the perfect square divided into further sequential squares of 1, 4, 9, 16, 25, 36, 49, 81 and up to 1024. This scheme, when implemented in town planning, is rigidly hierarchical. Each segment of the *mandala* is reserved for a particular caste: *brahmins* in the north, *kshatriyas* (or Rajputs) in the east, *vaishyas* (merchants) in the south, *shudras* (servants) in the west, with separate districts housing different trades.

to stay out of peak-hour traffic and have insect repellant to protect you from mosquitoes.

The design of the city followed a prescribed text on Hindu architecture – *Shilpa Shastra* – according to which all different parts should be contained within a grid-structure or *mandala*, encompassing blocks (seven in this case) divided by avenues. This is evident on street maps that depict the grid within the city walls, while modern Jaipur follows a random plan. Ten wall-gates survive today, contributing to the enchanting atmosphere of the pink city. The hectically busy **Badi Chaupar** crossroad is the heart of the commercial district, next to the Hawa Mahal. It lies in the middle of the main artery stretching from **Suraj Pol** (Sun Gate) in the east to **Chand Pol** (Moon Gate) in the west. Each block was designed to house a particular craft or activity – hence Suraj Pol Bazaar is the elephant owners' quarters, **Johari Bazaar** is a market for jewellery and cotton fabrics, **Bapu** and **Nehru Bazaars** for textiles, shoes and perfumes.

The three most important landmarks lie within the **City Palace complex** which forms the core of the beautiful Pink City.

Opposite: *Magnificent Jaipur City Palace.*
Right: *Hawa Mahal with its 953 latticed windows.*

Hawa Mahal ★★★

Unmissable and bizarre with its pink, highly ornamental decor-like appearance, the Hawa Mahal or Palace of Winds is not, and never was, much more than a splendid façade. Built in the last year of the 18th century by the poet-maharaja Sawai Pratap Singh for his wives, courtesans and their attendants, its purpose was to enable the women to observe city life and processions while remaining unseen in *purdah* (behind a veil). The five-storey sandstone building has 953 latticed windows and balconies constructed in such a way that the slightest breeze would cool the observers they concealed. Climbing the stairs you will realize that the edifice is only a room deep and has no solid back wall. Moreover, the top floor offers great views of the colourful, buzzing city streets below. Open 09:00–16:30 daily.

Jaipur City Palace ★★★

The royal family still live in a portion of the **Chandra Mahal** (Moon Palace) – though most of it, known as the City Palace Museum, has been open to the public since 1959. Visitors enter through the **Atish Pol** (Stable

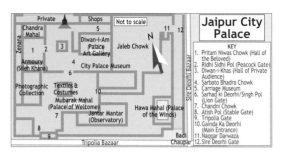

Jaipur City Palace

KEY
1. Pritam Niwas Chowk (Hall of the Beloved)
2. Ridhi Sidhi Pol (Peacock Gate)
3. Diwan-i-Khas (Hall of Private Audience)
4. Sarbato Bhadra Chowk
5. Carriage Museum
6. Sarhad ki Deorhi/Singh Pol (Lion Gate)
7. Chandni Chowk
8. Atish Pol (Stable Gate)
9. Tripolia Gate
10. Gainda Ka Deorhi (Main Entrance)
11. Naqqar Darwaza
12. Sire Deorhi Gate

Gate) or **Gainda Ka Deorhi**, if travelling from Hawa Mahal, while **Tripolia** (Three-arched) **Gate** is reserved for the royals. The first building you come across is the marble-and-sandstone **Mubarak Mahal** (Palace of Welcome) which was built by Madho Singh II (son of Jai Singh II) to receive foreign visitors. It is now a textile museum displaying the finest royal outfits in silk, muslin and cotton, embroidered coats, *pashmina* shawls and block-printed fabrics. The star of the collection is the pink, padded *atamsikh* (soul delighter) or quilted robe of Madho Singh I who stood 2.1m (7 feet) tall and weighed 225kg (500 pounds). There are also musical instruments and the toys of the princes and princesses, Jaipur blue pottery and Mughal glass. The building in the corner houses the impressive **Sileh Khana** (royal Rajput armoury), a collection of beautiful daggers, swords, spears and body armour inlaid with ivory, jade, silver and gold. There are also inscribed swords that belonged to Shah Jahan and Man Singh I, a Persian imperial sword and the turban-helmet worn by Jai Singh I in battle.

The stunning, marble-inlaid **Sarhad ki Deorhi**, also called Singh Pol (Lion Gate), was decorated with elephants carved out of a single piece of marble on the occasion of the current maharaja's birth in 1931. Through the brass-plated gates you enter the courtyard of the **Diwan-i-Khas** (Hall of Private Audience). Note the continuation of the Mughal trend of having separate buildings for different activities. Under its pink arches stand the two largest silver objects in the world, the vessels were made from 243kg (536 pounds) of silver and can hold up to 1182 litres (2080 pints). When Madho Singh II embarked on a voyage to England in 1901 to attend the coronation of King Edward VII, he chartered an ocean liner, built a temple on board, and set sail throwing bags

---

THE EXTRAVAGANCE OF THE RAJPUTS

The Rajputs, or Princes of Rajputana, never did anything in half measure. Their code of honour was rigid and extreme (it included practices such as self-immolation and blood feuds) and was what made them such outstanding warriors. Their architecture is often dream-like and fantastic, but also enduring and grand, as seen in the Jaipur City Palace, Amber Palace, the Hawa Mahal, the unique Jantar Mantar observatory and Rambagh Palace, and in Rajasthani palaces such as Gwalior Fort and Datia Palace (*see* pages 118–120). Rajput extravagance also manifested itself in parades and celebrations when the extraordinary wealth of the maharajas was put on display through elephants, jewellery, gold, and, in the 20th century, luxury cars. When Madho Singh II embarked on a voyage to England for the coronation of Edward VII, he threw bags of gold, silver and silk into Bombay harbour for propitious winds. Today, a glimpse of this glorious past can be seen at the Elephant Festival in Jaipur.

of gold, silver and silk into Mumbai harbour for good luck. He carried along these specially made silver vessels full of Ganges drinking water to avoid contamination from 'impure' foreign water.

To the right stands the **Diwan-i-Am**, formerly the Hall of Public Audience, now the Palace Art Gallery. The painted walls are hung with lush and rare Mughal carpets from Agra, Lahore and other places. Exhibits of interest include gold and silver thrones, glass chandeliers and miniatures from the Jaipur school and from the Mughal school. Passing through the Diwan-i-Khas courtyard again and through a small marble gateway in its left corner called **Ridhi Sidhi Pol**, you reach the wonderfully fancy **Pritam Niwas Chowk** (Hall of the Beloved), which is known as Peacock Courtyard due to the dazzling colours of the patterned decorations around the four doorways. It was built by the creator of the Hawa Mahal, Pratap Singh. Here, private music parties were held, observed by the royal harem from behind the latticed screens upstairs. Each of the four doors represents a season and is embellished with scenes from Krishna's life.

Beyond the courtyard lie the royal apartments that are closed to the public. Behind the palace, **Jai Niwas Bagh** gardens with the temple of **Govinda Deva** is popular with Hindu worshippers as well as peacocks and monkeys. Govinda is another name for Krishna when he is engaged in frolics with the gopis, his cowgirl-consorts. The temple was established by Jai Singh II who proclaimed Govinda the patron deity of Jaipur Rajputs. The City Palace is open daily from 09:30 to 16:45.

ANOKHI

Anokhi is a designer label created by an Indo-English couple in the 70s. It produces clothes, furnishing and accessories of high quality and simple originality, keeping its crafts people – weavers, dyers, printers – in employment throughout the year. The company has also actively been involved in Rajasthan's cultural and natural heritage preservation, charity and drought relief projects. There are Anokhi outlets in Santushti Shopping Centre and Khan Market in New Delhi and in Tilak Marg, southwest of the Pink City (see map on page 63)

Below *Giant silver vessel at the City Palace.*

Jantar Mantar ★★★

At first glance what looks like a futuristic sculpture park is in fact an ambitious and unique astronomical observatory. *Jantra* means instrument, *mantra* magic formula – but there is more science here than magic. The first open-air observatory in India was built earlier in Delhi by Jai Singh II, followed by other ones in Ujjain, Varanasi and Mathura. This Jantar Mantar is the largest and the only one made of stone. The gifted maharaja, Jai Singh II, was very much *au fait* with the latest trends in European science when construction began and was determined to build the most accurate instruments for measuring time in Hindustan. The 13 devices are complex and to get a grasp of the basic concepts you may want to hire a guide, available at the entrance, or refer to the brochure you will be given. Below is a summary of the main instruments.

Nari Yantra is a sundial consisting of two cylinders placed at an angle; the one to the north was used in winter, the other in summer. **Samrat Yantra** (supreme instrument) is the most imposing construction in the grounds, standing at 27m (90 feet). It is a giant sundial for measuring local time in hours, minutes and seconds. It also measures meridian time, zenith distance and the

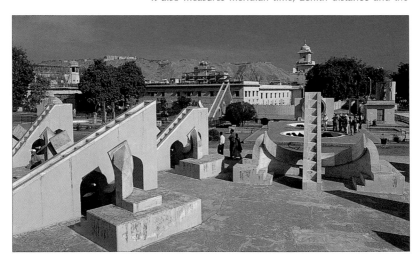

altitude of celestial spheres. The local time was announced to the people of Jaipur with drums sounded at the top of the instrument's stairs. It is listed as the largest sundial in the *Guinness Book of Records*.

Rashi Valaya Yantra is a group of twelve instruments that correspond to the zodiac signs. They are more for fun than serious scientific purposes. **Jai Prakash Yantra** was Jai Singh's invention, which consists of two large concave marble spheres representing the celestial sphere upside-down. Their rims represent the horizon and are graduated at 360 degrees. Its function is to determine local time and the sun's path. **Ram Yantra** and **Digamsha Yantra** – huge circular devices – are compasses of a sort used to calculate azimuths (distances of celestial bodies) and altitudes. The **Yantra Raj** is an ancient metal astrolabe designed by Jai Singh. Its surface is inscribed with a diagram of the cosmos and it was used to calculate the height and position of celestial objects. It too, features in the *Guinness Book of Records* as the largest astrolabe in the world. Open 09:00–16:30 daily.

Above: *Nari Yantra, a sundial at Jantar Mantar*
Opposite: *Jantar Mantar observatory conceived by the genius of Jai Singh II.*

JAI SINGH I AND JAI SINGH II

Mirza Raja Jai Singh I ascended the Amber throne at the tender age of 12, just like Jai Singh II, some 80 years later. Both rajas were favourites of the Mughal emperors. Jai Singh I rose to the absolute height of power and was given an army of 7000 by the emperor, an unprecedented act of trust between Mughals and Rajputs. Jai Singh I was responsible for most of what stands today of the magnificent Amber Palace. Jai Singh II, a precocious child-ruler, surpassed his namesake in talents and successes, and remained in favour with Aurangzeb until the emperor's death which marked the end of the golden age of the Mughal-Rajput union.

The Bazaars of Jaipur ★★★

The crafts of Jaipur constitute the city's economic back bone. The variety of products, density and size of the bazaars, uniqueness of some crafts and finesse of the artisans' work all make for an unmissable experience for the connoisseur as well as for the idle stroller. Jaipur is paradise for the compulsive shopper but also for the aesthete. Allow plenty of time to look for the best value and quality. If your time is very limited, make a trip to the **Rajasthan Government Handicrafts Emporium** on the Amber Road which is a reliable, fixed-price showcase of local crafts. Do not, however, trust the 'Government approved' sign outside various other shops along MI Road and Amber Road, although many have great stock.

The most obvious place to start is the tourist shopping area around Hawa Mahal, where you can buy anything from curios to gems – beware though, as this is definitely not the place to look for top quality or authenticity. **Johari Bazaar**, the oldest and liveliest market of the city, is a long succession of temples, grocers and gem dealers. Here, and along Gopalji Ka Bazaar off Johari Bazaar, is the lapidary centre of Jaipur – and indeed of India. You can watch cutters and polishers at their delicate craft, known as *meenakari*: the characteristic Jaipuri style of gem-inlaid gold. Do your homework before buying and go to a reputable dealer to make sure your diamonds are not zircon. Sapphires, rubies and emeralds are all very cheap and jewellery can be made to your own design. The established shop of **Bhuramal Rajmal Surana**, in a beautiful old *haveli* in Haldion ka Rasta (another lane off Johari Bazaar), is where some of the best designs and quality can be found. MI Road has a number of jewellers of which the most reliable is **Gem Palace** where the client's design can be made on the spot. Interesting silver jewellery can be found in Chameli Market opposite the Post Office in MI Road.

Jaipur and the nearby town of Sanganer are world-famous exporters of **textiles**. Tie-dye fabrics and **block-prints** are found in Johari Bazaar and you can see the dyers and printers at work in the district north of Ramganj Bazaar. **Arawali Textiles** off Amber Road is only one of many excellent textile shops where you can get clothes made for you from silk or cotton at a fraction of the European price. Take a garment or picture for the tailor to copy. There is a cluster of Rajasthani cloth shops in narrow lanes on the western side of Johari Bazaar, near Badi Chaupar. Good shops outside of the Pink City include **Anokhi** on Tilak Marg, southwest of MI Road, which has expensive Western-style clothes and **Maharaja Textile Printer** near Gangapol, the northern gate of the walled city. For more – and a closer look at the techniques – travel to **Sanganer**, 16km (10 miles) away (*see* page 86), also the home of handmade paper.

Opposite: *Jootis for sale in the streets of Jaipur.*
Below: *Puppets wait for customers in Deorhi Bazaar.*

BLUE POTTERY

Blue pottery came to India with the first Mughal Babur. A Persian concept combined with Chinese glazing technique, blue tiles became part of Mughal architecture. The method was kept secret and an ever-diminishing number of craftsmen were privy to it, until it disappeared altogether. Only recently has it been revived by Kripal Singh, who travelled the world to rediscover this ancient technique and restore it to India. His studio is in west Jaipur and his apprentices work all over the area.

Opposite: *Sari seller in Johari Bazaar.*
Below: *Bangles for sale at a Jaipur bazaar.*

Leading to the east from the frantic and highly entertaining **Badi Chaupar**, the heart of the city where mass-produced items can be found, is **Ramganj Bazaar**, that specializes in traditional slip-on shoes and slippers known as *jootis*, These are mostly made of leather and sometimes embroidered. The best ones are made of camel hide. **Mojri**, Bhawani Villa, Gulab Path, tel: (0141) 237 7037, is an excellent guaranteed leather outlet. North of Badi Chaupar is **Sire Deorhi Bazaar** where puppets are made and sold. If you haven't visited the **City Palace** yet, this is a good way: go through the **Sire Deorhi Gate** and into **Jaleb Chowk** square where you can have a refreshing drink at a café.

A unique craft flourishing here is the Jaipur blue pottery and tiles. The man who revived this ancient craft from the neglect of recent history is **Kripal Singh Shekhawat** whose studio is to the west of the Pink City, B-18a Shiva Marg, Bani Park, tel: (0141) 220 1127 – call for an appointment. You will need to take a taxi or auto-rickshaw there. His characteristic use of aquamarine blues and saturated colours, in addition to the classic blue and white tiles, is a pleasure for the eye. He also offers tourists lessons in pottery and miniature-painting. An offspring of blue pottery is **ceramic jewellery**, found in Neerja on Bhawani Singh Marg off Sawai Ram Singh Road in the south.

Other crafts well worth seeing are beautiful handmade paper, available at **Khadi Ghar** in MI Road; the intricate brassware enamelling at **PM Allah Buksh & Son** on MI Road; and sandalwood carving, miniature-painting and marble sculpture in **Khazane Wallon ka Rasta** off Chand Pol Bazaar.

Other popular bazaars are **Nehru Bazaar** and **Bapu Bazaar**, alongside the southern gates of the Pink City, selling bangles, local perfumes, block-printed cottons and shoes. **Tripolia Bazaar** west of Badi Chaupar and **Chaura Bazaar** which runs off it, sell textiles and more mundane objects. A note of caution: it is always safest to pay in cash, but if you have to pay by credit card, make sure you don't lose sight of your card. Scams have been known to occur here, especially in the gem trade.

Rajasthani Food

Rajasthani cuisine is characterized by two extremes: non-vegetarian at one end and strictly vegetarian at the other. Although eating out is a relatively recent phenomenon, the city's restaurants and hotels cater for both tastes. Entire communities, such as the Jains, are traditionally vegetarian. However, Rajput diet through the centuries has focused on meat. Mughlai cuisine, influenced by Mughal tastes and widely available in Jaipur, is also meat oriented. A typical Rajput meat dish consists of mutton, usually lamb or goat, roasted or minced, from which *keema* and *kebabs* are made. Probably the most appealing to visitors would be *sulla*, marinated lamb grilled on a skewer. Fish, white meat, pork, rabbit and partridge are also on the menus. Richness of flavours and an abundance of spices characterizes most Rajasthani meat dishes, although there are milder variations such as yoghurt-based seasoning. The staple food of the common people is *bajre ki roti* (millet bread), usually eaten with onions and chutney.

JEWELLERY

The women of Rajasthan are noted for their colourful clothes and heavy, elaborate jewellery. Some of the most brilliant silver jewellery is worn by the Banjaras or gypsy nomads. It is very fashionable in the cities – the heavy silver belts, bangles and anklets are copied by many fashion designers in Delhi and Bombay. Aside from the aesthetic value of adornment, there is an economic reason why women choose to wear kilograms worth of silver: it is a portable form of wealth. In the past, carrying one's wealth to protect it from looters was a very sensible thing indeed!

A fancier meal might include *jhal* (potato curry) and fried white bread. Jaipur has a number of excellent vegetarian restaurants among them are **LMB**, **Chanakya**, **Four Seasons** – and some very good non-vegetarian ones like **Chowki Dhani** (22km [14 miles] out of town but worth the trip), **Niro's** and the **Copper Chimney**. The top hotels such as **Jai Mahal** and the **Rajputana Palace Sheraton** also have outstanding restaurants, some with outdoor dining and Indian music (*see* page 79).

BEYOND THE PINK CITY

If you have an extra day, have a look at wider Jaipur. It provides welcome respite from the hectic pace of the city. Gardens, museums, cenotaphs, pavilions and temples all lie outside the walled city.

Ram Niwas Gardens ★★★

Just outside New Gate, lie the gardens of Maharaja Ram Singh who, inspired by the worldliness of then capital Calcutta, undertook the construction of the site as a famine charity project in 1868. They house the magnificent **Albert Hall**, also known as Central Museum, and one of the first zoos in the country. The project was initially conceived to provide relief for the famine that followed one drought and it soon became the cultural hub of the city. On the way to Albert Hall you will pass the Gallery of Modern Art and a crocodile breeding farm which is part of the zoo, but in poor condition. Albert Hall, a fine colonial building, was inspired by the grandeur of the Victoria and Albert Museum in London and combines Indo-Saracenic motifs and Victorian styles. Today it houses the **Central Museum** (open

10:00–16:30 daily, except Friday), exhibiting local customs and crafts. In a separate room, the Durbar Hall displays rare carpets, including one of the most stunning ever made anywhere: a 17th-century Persian garden carpet whose colours are still vivid. Its design was based on the idea of the *charbagh* (*see* panel on page 103) or pleasure garden.

Sisodia Rani ka Bagh

Passing through the southeast Ghat Gate and taking the road to Agra, you will reach **Vidyadharji ka Bagh** (about 8km [5 miles] from the city), a garden dedicated to the genius architect of Jaipur and the only remaining memorial to his life and achievement. Opposite it is the **Sisodia Rani ka Bagh**, a landscaped garden and country palace (one of the most beautiful in Rajasthan) built by Jai Singh II for one of his wives – a Rajput princess from the Sisodia clan whom he had married to strengthen political alliances. When relations between Jai Singh II and the Sisodia Rajputs deteriorated, the queen was exiled to a private residence outside the City Palace with her son

Opposite: *Charcoal-grilled sullas, a favourite Rajasthani speciality.*
Below: *The splendid Albert Hall.*

HANUMAN, THE MONKEY-GOD

Monkeys – like elephants – have special status in India. Hanuman temples are widespread and overrun with the noisy creatures. Hanuman was the chief consort of King Rama in the *Ramayana* epic. He is also the patron of wrestlers and acrobats and, strangely, credited with the invention of Sanskrit grammar.

Opposite: *Rambagh Palace, now one of India's most sumptuous hotels.*
Below: *Sisodia Rani ka Bagh, built by Jai Singh II for his Rajput wife.*

Madho Singh. The gardens are open 08:00–18:00, the palace is usually closed and can only be seen from the outside, but ask the guard to open up for you – it still retains the lush atmosphere of a regal retreat.

Galta Temples

The temples at **Galta** can be reached by the road leaving from Suraj Pol to the east, or by driving on north from Sisodia Rani ka Bagh. First on the way is the **Hanuman Temple** – dedicated to the monkey god. The place is overrun with monkeys which are at their loudest and happiest when the Hanuman priest arrives at 16:00 in a rickshaw with sacks of bananas for their daily feast. Hanuman is one of the most popular Hindu deities. Further up the road are the water tanks – the upper used for bathing by people, the lower by monkeys which have a protected status anywhere in proximity to a Hanuman temple. Although they are friendly, avoid playing with them and giving them food as they can carry rabies. The **Galta temples** are 250 years old and painted with entertaining religious scenes. There are beautiful views over the surrounding plains.

Gaitor Tombs

Some 4km (2 miles) off the main road to Amber and 6km (3 miles) from the City Palace are the marble **chhatris** (small, domed Mughal kiosks) or mausolea of Jaipur's rulers. The finest of them all is of course that of Jai Singh II, built by his son and successor Iswari Singh. It depicts Hindu mythological scenes and some of Jaipur's landmarks including the Hawa Mahal. Iswari Singh himself was an ineffective ruler who took his life by swallowing poison and have a cobra bite him just to be sure. This suicide was prompted by the advance of the fierce Marathas – a tribe forever at war with the Rajputs. The maharaja's wives also responded: some took poison and the remaining 21 committed *sati* (self-immolation) on their husband's funeral pyre – which was a hasty affair, hence the absence of a tomb for this unfortunate ruler.

Man Sagar Lake

This lake is a 10 minute drive travelling north from Gaitor Tombs, so it is best to stop by on your way to Amber or into Jaipur. One passes factory shops making and selling block-print, carpets, pottery and other fabrics. The now inaccessible romantic palace in the middle of the lake, Jal Mahal, was built by Jai Singh II's son Madho Singh I and used for duck shooting parties.

RAMBAGH PALACE HOTEL

This palace began in the early 19th century as four pavilions that were turned into a hunting resort by Ram Singh and renamed Rambagh after him. Madho Singh's 11-year-old son Man Singh was kept and educated here, under British tutelage, away from the bad influences of the City Palace. Here, in 1931, the first male Rajput child in 100 years was born, an event that was celebrated with due pomp. Around that time, Man Singh met and fell in love with the 13-year-old daughter of a neighbouring maharaja. She was Gayatri Devi – known as one of the most beautiful women of her time who became his wife eight years later. The palace was aggrandized for this occasion. The queen survived her husband who died in a polo accident and now lives in the Lily Pool Palace on the Rambagh grounds. Following Independence, in 1957, the palace was turned into the most sumptuous hotel of its kind in India, now run by the Taj Group of Hotels.

Jaipur at a Glance

Jaipur has hot and humid summers and chilly winters. In winter (Oct–Mar) the days are sunny and pleasant but at night temperatures can drop to as low as 5°C. Also, winter evenings can be foggy. Nonetheless, the best time to visit Jaipur is **October–March**. March is also the time of the fabulous **Elephant Festival**, a sight to behold.

The **railway station** is 1km west of the central city; rail information tel: 131, reservations 135, www.indianrail.gov.in The **bus terminus** is closer, in Station Road; coach information, tel: (0141) 511 6031, reservations (0141) 220 5790. If **driving**, you'll probably arrive from the north, through Amber. Domestic **flights** are from Delhi, Mumbai, Kolkata, Ahmedabad, Jodhpur and Udaipur, and an international flight from Dubai; for details, visit www.indian-airlines.nic.in www.jetairways.com www.jetlite.com Sanganer Airport is 16km south of Jaipur.

Taxis and auto-rickshaws are the best transport. In smaller and cluttered areas, such as the bazaars within the walled city, cycle-rickshaws are a good option. You will need to bargain them down or use the pre-paid rank beside the bus station. It is worth hiring a good driver by the day or

half day. Heavy pollution and dusty wind blowing in from the Thar Desert in the summer can cause throat and lung problems so use taxis with air-conditioning. Within the Pink City, peak-hour traffic is horrendous and best avoided.

Jaipur is best known for its regal accommodation – former palaces transformed into spectacular hotels that rate among the most original in the country. The less expensive *haveli* (town-house style) accommodation consists of refurbished noble mansions. While not always cheap, by Western standards, they are good value. There are also some budget options. Hotels are heavily booked around festival times, so it is best to book in advance.

LUXURY

Sheraton Rajputana Palace Hotel Jaipur, Palace Rd, Jaipur, tel: (0141) 510 0100; www.starwoodhotels.com A large super deluxe modern *haveli*-style hotel, with a pool, superb restaurants including the North-West Frontier Peshawari, a blow-out buffet at the Jal Mahal, and wonderful ice-creams in the coffee shop. Central. Also has an excellent bookshop, Bookwise (India) PVT Ltd, tel: (0141) 510 7255. **Rambagh Palace** (*see* page 77), Bhawani Singh Road, Jaipur, tel: (0141) 221 1919, e-mail: rambagh.jaipur@tajhotels.com

Glorious palace-hotel, the former residence of the maharajas of Jaipur. Huge gardens, polo grounds, shops, restaurant. The suites are out of this world – and so are the prices. Cultural performances at night. **Oberoi Rajvilas**, Goner Road, Jaipur; tel: (0141) 268 0101, gm@oberoi-rajvilas.com www.rajvilas.com Oberoi's luxurious Moghul fort, set in lush gardens; separate villas (with private pools) and tents as well as rooms. Elephant and horseback treks arranged.

MID-RANGE

Samode Haveli, Gangapole, tel: (0141) 263 2407, www.samode.com Gorgeous, lushly decorative former residence of the Rawals of Samode. Impeccable service, restaurant; recommended. **Shahpura House**, Devi Marg, tel: (0141) 220 2293, www.shahpurahouse.com A fanciful wedding cake of a house. Rooftop restaurant, air conditioning, and bathrooms in all rooms. Near station. **Alsisar Haveli**, Sansar Chandra Road, tel: (0141) 236 8290, www.alsisar.com Restored *haveli*, pool, terrace, good restaurant. Puppet and dance shows in the evening.

BUDGET

Arya Niwas, Sansar Chandra Road, tel: (0141) 237 2456; www.aryaniwas.com Efficiently run, all the basics. Good, reasonable vegetarian restaurant. Internet access.

Bissau Palace, Outside Chandpole, tel: (0141) 230 4391; www.bissaupalace.com Atmospherically faded former residence of the Thakurs of Bissau, still run by their descendants; 28 rooms, gardens, badminton and tennis courts, pool and restaurant.

Diggi Palace, Diggi House, SMS Hospital Road, tel: (0141) 237 3091; e-mail: reservations @hoteldiggipalace.com Converted *haveli* in lovely garden near the SMS Hospital. Best are the detached cottages on the lawn. Good restaurant.

WHERE TO EAT

Most of the best restaurants are in the hotels; try those in the Rajputana Palace Sheraton. Good hotels with excellent restaurants include the Jai Mahal Palace Hotel, Jacob Rd, which has veranda and lawn tables, and top *Mughlai* and North Indian cuisine; the Mansingh Hotel, off Sansar Chandra Marg, where there is outstanding Indian food, rooftop dining and *qawwali* singing (see panel page 52).

Chokhi Dhani, Tonk Road, 19km south of Jaipur, tel: (0141) 277 0555. Popular among wealthy locals, excellent Rajasthani food. Small entrance fee for the live entertainment. Open Mon–Sat 18:30–23:00, Sun to 14:30.

Copper Chimney, Mirza Ismail Road, tel: (0141) 237 2275. *Mughlai* and North Indian cuisine, additional Western and Chinese menus.

Dasaprakash, 5 Kamal Mansions, Mirza Ismail Road (opp. Sagar Department Store). Branch of widespread chain. Vegetarian South Indian and continental food, plus an ice cream parlour.

Four Seasons, D-43A2 Subhash Marg, tel: (0141) 237 5450. In residential district, very popular and cheap. Has great South and North Indian dishes, ice creams and shakes.

Niro's, MI Road, top-notch Indian food, plus vegetarian dishes and other options.

Chanakya, MI Road, tel: (0141) 237 6161. Popular restaurant, Continental and Indian. Open for lunch and dinner.

LMB, Johari Bazaar, tel: (0141) 256 5844. Hugely successful, it prides itself on its pure Brahmin cooking: no garlic or onions. The ingredients are allegedly all ground and mixed on the premises, and everything is cooked in *ghee* (clarified butter). Also has traditional desserts including mango and pistachio ice creams.

Lassiwalla, across from Niro's, MI Road. Popular in the summer, unmissable refreshment stop. *Lassi* is a delicious yoghurt drink, served sweet or salted.

Mr Beans, E-141A, C-Scheme, Sardar Patel Marg, tel: (0141) 222 3650. The place to hang out if you are desperate for a latte, popular with local yuppies. Coffee in 26 flavours!

TOURS AND EXCURSIONS

Full- and half-day tours of Jaipur and environs are a good option. Book these, or your own government-approved guide, through your hotel, through the **Rajasthan Tourist Office** at the railway station (Platform 1) and at the Tourist Hotel, MI Road, tel: (0141) 511 0598 (open 08:00–20:00), or through the **Government of India Tourist Office**, MI Road, tel: (0141) 511 0597, or State Hotel, Khasa Kothi, tel: (0141) 237 2200, e-mail: indtourjpr@raj.nic.in

USEFUL CONTACTS

Police, tel: 100.

SMS Hospital, Sawai Ram Singh Marg, tel: (0141) 256 0291.

Thomas Cook (for currency exchange), A-B2 (102) Jaipur Towers, Mirza Ismail Road, tel: (0141) 236 0940 or 236 0974 or 236 0001, fax: (0141) 360 974. There are also plenty of ATM machines.

JAIPUR	J	F	M	A	M	J	J	A	S	O	N	D
AVERAGE TEMP. °C	14	17	23	29	34	35	31	30	30	27	21	16
AVERAGE TEMP. °F	57	63	73	84	93	95	88	86	86	81	70	61
HOURS SUN DAILY	12	12	12	14	14	14	13	14	13	12	12	12
RAINFALL mm	14	8	9	4	10	54	193	239	90	19	3	4
RAINFALL in	0.5	0.3	0.4	0.2	0.4	2.1	7.5	9.3	3.5	0.7	0.1	0.2

4
Around Jaipur

Jaipur is the capital of a state that abounds with interesting sights well worth the detour. As in the rest of India, distances in Rajasthan are too vast to enable quick access to some of the other fascinating towns, but the places listed below are all within half a day's road travel (at the most). Among these are some spectacular **natural reserves** rich in animal and birdlife, including tigers, crocodiles, cranes and eagles. There are craft villages and **palaces**. The highlight among these is the fort-palace of **Amber** (open 09:00–16:00 daily).

AMBER FORT-PALACE

Overlooking a lake from an impregnable hill, the yellow **Amber Fort-Palace** is 11km (7 miles) north of Jaipur. One of the most majestic hilltop forts in Rajasthan, and perhaps all of India, it was the ultimate seat of Rajput power and a symbol of opulence. Begun by one aesthetic maharaja and finished by another, its peak of glory in the 16th and 17th centuries coincided with the flourishing of the Rajput-Mughal alliance.

The **Kachhawaha Rajputs** who claimed descent from one of the sons of lord Rama, took over Amber after defeating the previous tribal rulers, the **Susawat Minas**, in the mid-12th century. It was not until the 16th century, however, that Amber fort came into existence. The enlightened Mughal emperor Akbar forged friendly relations with the proud Rajputs by marrying the daughter of the then ruler of Amber thus marking the beginning of centuries of prosperity in Rajputana. Amber rulers were given positions of

DON'T MISS

*** Amber Fort-Palace: situated on a hill it offers panoramic views of Maota Lake and the old town below.
*** National parks: enjoy a tiger safari and admire scenery at **Ranthambhore** and **Sariska**.
** Jaigarh and **Nahargarh forts:** great views.
** Samode Palace: stay in this luxurious hotel.
** Alwar: visit the palace.
* Sanganer: noted for its fine block-printed textiles and paper.

Opposite: *The south end of Amber Fort-Palace with Jaigarh Fort on the hill.*

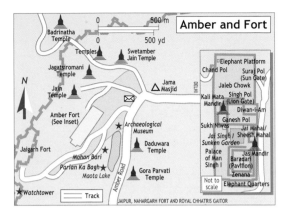

Amber and Fort

Badrinatha Temple
Temples
Jagatsiromani Temple
Swetamber Jain Temple
N
Jain Temple
Jama Masjid
Amber Fort (See Inset)
Archaeological Museum
Jaigarh Fort
Daduwara Temple
Mohan Bari
Partan Ka Bagh
Gora Parvati Temple
Maota Lake
Watchtower
Track
0   500 m
0   500 yd

Elephant Platform
Chand Pol   Suraj Pol (Sun Gate)
Jaleb Chowk
Kali Mata   Singh Pol (Lion Gate)
Mandir   Diwan-i-Am
                 Ganesh Pol
Sukh Niwas   Jai Mahal/
Jai Singh I   Sheesh Mahal
Sunken Garden
Palace of Man   Jas Mandir
Singh I   Baradari (Pavilion)
                 Zenana
Not to scale   Elephant Quarters

JAIPUR, NAHARGARH FORT AND ROYAL CHHATRIS GAITOR

power in the Mughal court and army. With the incredible wealth accumulated as a result, Maharaja Man Singh built the first palace of Amber, now at the back end of the complex, and a shrine to the goddess Kali that is still in use today. A great patron of the arts, Man Singh established a thriving community of craftsmen who specialized in ceramics, block-printing, enamelling and paper-making – a tradition that lives on in Amber and Jaipur.

Half a century later Jai Singh I, who ascended the throne of Amber at the age of 12, expanded the palace into what forms the glorious front section of the complex today. The Mughal architectural and cultural influence can be seen clearly in many aspects of the palace, such as the mirror inlay, the double-bracket supports on pavilion-like buildings, and the cooling water system inside, making it a visual celebration of a mighty political and cultural alliance. The shift of the Rajput seat of power from Agra to Jaipur in the 18th century is similar to that of the Mughal throne moving from Agra to Delhi in the 17th.

From the small tourist complex on the main Amber road, access to the fort towering above is by foot, elephant or car. Of these, the most dignified – if it isn't too hot – is the pleasant fifteen-minute hike up the winding stairs occupied by buskers, beggars and pigs. If you want to sit on an elephant, you can do so in the main courtyard of the fort, **Jaleb Chowk**, which is entered through the **Suraj Pol** (Sun Gate) that is a reminder of the divine provenance of the Kachhawahas. Before passing through **Singh Pol** (Lion Gate) at the top of the stairs and into the palace complex, take a peek at **Kali Mata Mandir** to the right. This is a temple to Sila Mata, yet

KALI, GODDESS OF WAR

Kali, the Hindu goddess of war and destruction, is an aspect of Durga, herself an aspect of Parvati, Shiva's consort. Kali is most often portrayed with four arms (Durga has 10), skulls hanging around her neck and blood dripping from her mouth. Sometimes she dances on the body of Shiva or of vanquished demons. Animal sacrifices to Kali were common practice in Rajputana, performed in order to pacify her wrath. The last maharaja of Jaipur, Man Singh II, would occasionally drive in his jeep to Kali Mata Mandir at Amber to sacrifice a live goat.

another incarnation of the bloodthirsty goddess, Kali, who was popular with the Rajputs. It was built by Man Singh I in 1604 and is still in use. The second courtyard's main feature is the stunning, red sandstone Mughal-style **Diwan-i-Am** (Hall of Public Audience), the most ambitious addition by Jai Singh. The third and largest gate, **Ganesh Pol**, which leads into the private apartments, is a magnificent building in itself and a triumph of the Rajasthani and Mughal decorative blend: painted floral motifs, images of gods, glass mosaics (possibly modelled on the Mughal tile-work) and *jaali* (carved screens) above the gate, through which the royal ladies observed the activities of the court. A diminutive, plump Ganesh, the elephant god of prosperity and happiness, is painted above the entrance. The courtyard has a landscaped, Mughal-style *charbagh* garden. To the right is **Sukh Niwas** (House of Pleasure), equipped with a system of fountains, where the royals retired on hot days. It was said to have the most beautiful among Rajput decorations. To the left is **Jai Mahal** (Hall of Victory), the royal

THE HALL OF PUBLIC AUDIENCE

The Diwan-i-Am at the Amber palace is unmistakably Mughal in style, reminiscent of those in Agra, Delhi and Fatehpur Sikri. The concept of having separate buildings for different activities is also Mughal, and is again seen in the City Palace in Jaipur.

Below: *Amber Fort-Palace, Ganesh Pol, a triumph of decorative art.*

GUNPOWDER

Gunpowder was a secret jealously kept by the Mughals. It had enabled them to defeat the Lodi sultans in the early 16th century and keep the Rajputs in submission. However, during his post as governor of Kabul for the Mughal emperor Akbar I in the late 16th century, Man Singh I gained access to the formula and brought it back to Amber. Much to the displeasure of the Mughals, cannons began to be made by the Rajputs.

private rooms. At ground level is the most splendid room of the palace – the **Sheesh Mahal** (Mirror Hall). Its marble walls and ceiling are inlaid with small pieces of mirror and coloured glass among bursts of floral engravings, creating the dazzling impression of a room full of jewels. Upstairs is Jai Singh's private apartment, **Jas Mandir** (Temple of Glory). Intricately decorated with mosaics and with a view to Lake Maota below, it has exquisite alabaster *jaali* at floor level. A climb up to the second storey of Ganesh Pol reveals a view to the courtyard below through the latticed screens where the royal harem once sat and observed.

The palace of Man Singh I lies through a small doorway at the far end of the gardens. He built 12 apartments or *zenana* (women's quarters) one for each of his wives, situated all around this fourth and last courtyard. Some remaining blue tile-work and paintings on the walls give an indication of the extent of the decorative work carried out under his orders.

Below: *The exquisite interior of Nahargarh Fort.*

NAHARGARH FORT

Also known as Tiger Fort, **Nahargarh** (floodlit at night) is close to the royal *chhatris* at Galta, along a ridgeroad off Amber Road that offers great views of the romantic duck-hunting pavilion, Jal Mahal, in Man Sagar Lake. The fort was built by Jai Singh II in 1734 as a defence post for the brand-new city of Jaipur. Here, where local time was announced with gunshots, the royal ladies came to cool off during summer (in the mid-19th century Ram Singh built more apartments for his wives). The

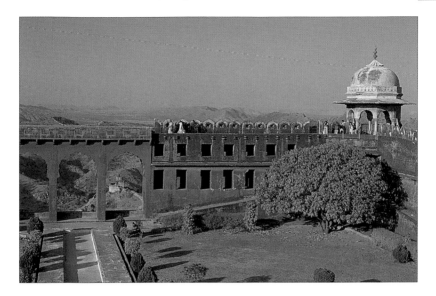

spectacular views over Jaipur and the fine decorations in the halls are well worth the effort. Open from 10:00–22:00 daily. There is also a small restaurant and a rest room at the top of the fort.

JAIGARH FORT

South of Amber Fort is the older fort of **Jaigarh**, home of the Kachhawaha rulers before Amber was built. The Kachhawaha treasure was kept here – ironically the treasurers were the defeated Meenas, previous lords of Amber. Only the maharaja's family had access to the fort. Here is found the largest cannon in India, **Jai Van** (Voice of Victory), whose barrel is decorated with elephants, birds and flowers. Built by Jai Singh II, it needed 100kg (221 pounds) of gun powder for each shot and when tested, the ball was found 38km (24 miles) away; this was the first and last time it was ever used. For those interested in weapons, the foundry – unique in India – is fully equipped with moulds, a kiln and more cannons on display. The palace has several halls and offers spectacular views. Open 09:00–16:30 daily.

Above: *Jaigarh Fort offers breathtaking views.*

THE KACHHAWAHA TREASURE

The unimaginable treasure of the Kachhawaha Rajputs was kept in their former residence Jaigarh Fort, where it was loyally guarded by their defeated enemies, the Meenas. Out of this wealth were born the palaces of Amber and Jaipur. Each newly appointed ruler was brought to the treasury blindfolded and allowed to take just one object for himself. Madho Singh II picked up a bird made from solid gold, with rubies for eyes and a large emerald in its beak. Attempts to excavate the buried treasure have been fruitless.

Right: *Block-printing is done using wooden blocks dipped in dye and printed onto cloth.*

SANGANER

This town 16km (10 miles) south of Jaipur is a hub of **textile production**, block-printing in particular being its trademark. Here you can watch the practice of an age-old tradition of handmade fabrics and designs – and purchase them at lower prices. Fabric is soaked in vats of hot dye, stirred, drained, then rinsed, sometimes soaked in cow dung to aid bleaching, and finally spread out in the sun for three days. Block-printing is a simple technique consisting of repetitively applying different-shaped wooden blocks to the fabric after dipping them in dye. The skill is in the precision of the application and the equal colouring of each print. While some producers prefer to use cheaper commercial chemicals, others, such as the famous label Anokhi, stick to natural vegetable dyes. Most textile shops are found along the main road. In addition, there are workshops making beautiful paper from the cotton and silk left-overs of the textile industry and hand-printed pottery in blue, white and green. There are a number of Jain and Krishna temples in the town.

RANTHAMBHORE NATIONAL PARK

Nowhere in India are you more likely to spot a tiger than in the Ranthambhore National Park, some 161km (100 miles) south of Jaipur. Due to the constant proximity of jeeps filled with tiger-watchers, these most majestic of animals are not shy; sometimes they will hunt, drink from one of the marshy lakes, or simply lounge about while crowds of avid tourists snap pictures of them. At present it is estimated that there are about 45 tigers at Ranthambhore, but as the reserve is quite large, seeing one is not guaranteed and you may have to try more than once. At least one overnight stay is recommended. January to April is the best time to try, as this is the dry season when tigers come out to the lakes. The park has a wealth of other animals – leopard (more difficult to spot), jackal, chital, crested serpent eagle, deer, sloth bear, wild boar and crocodile. The latter can be spotted in the marshes on the side of the road, where ruined, moss-covered temples rise out of stagnant waters as if out of a dream. The park was once used as hunting grounds by Rajput rulers seated on elephants.

SAMODE PALACE

Approximately 42km (26 miles) north of Jaipur, west of the main road to Delhi, stands the yellow, decadent 18th century palace-hotel of Samode. It rose to fame in the late 1980s when a romantic film, *The Far Pavilions,* was shot here. It is situated in the midst of bare hills topped with forts and is ideal for a night's retreat, complete with candlelight rooftop dinner. The lords of Samode, loyal to the rulers of Jaipur, traced their origins to a prince of the Kachhawaha Rajputs and the youngest heirs still own the palace. The glittering **Sheesh Mahal** is reminiscent of its

> **BROTHERLY INTRIGUE**
>
> Sanganer was where Jai Singh II and his power-hungry half-brother Vijay Singh met, in the presence of their mother, to reach an agreement over Vijay's claims to the throne of Amber. The queen mother's courtiers, however, turned out to be disguised soldiers. No sooner had Jai Singh promised to fulfil his brother's demands, than Vijay found himself locked away in a room. Jai Singh II proceeded to create the city of Jaipur, becoming the most distinguished scholar, scientist, humanist and aesthete of all Rajput rulers.

Below: *A tiger lying at Ranthambhore National Park and Tiger Reserve.*

THE ELEPHANT GOD

Ganesh, the good-natured, elephant-headed son of Shiva and Parvati, is a symbol of knowledge, good fortune and success. The most popular deity among Hindus, his image is ubiquitous throughout India. Jaipur's Elephant Festival is a spectacular event, during which the bejewelled beasts parade through the city to the sound of drums. The elephants which transport tourists at Amber belong to special elephant unions.

namesake at Amber palace. The village of Samode produces tie-and-dye and block-printed fabrics, miniature painting and lacquered bangles.

SARISKA NATIONAL PARK

Similar to Ranthambhore, Sariska National Park is home to a current estimate of about 25 tigers, as well as chital, wild boar, mongoose, and a variety of birds. There is a temple to Hanuman and the atmospheric ruins were once buildings used by the maharaja hunters. It is an alternative to the more famous Ranthambhore Reserve, depending on which way you are travelling.

ALWAR

If you stop to see Sariska, Alwar is only 37km (23 miles) north on the way to Delhi and worth taking a couple of hours to explore. The **City Palace**, set on huge lush grounds, holds a **museum** and has a view of the large tank surrounded by elegant *ghats* and three-storeyed pavilions. There is also a fine marble-and-sandstone cenotaph **Moosi Maharani ki Chhatri**, that was built to commemorate the *sati* (self-immolation by fire) carried out on a local ruler's funeral pyre by his mistress. At night, the gates of the palace used to be closed to protect the town from tigers.

Right: *Elephant polo was a sport that was favoured by maharajas.*

Around Jaipur at a Glance

For information on the climate in this region, see page 78.

Amber, Jaigarh and Nawalgarh are easily reached by **car**. **Buses** to these forts, as well as to all the other destinations in this chapter, leave Jaipur every day; buses to Amber leave from the Hawa Mahal every 30 mins. If comfort is a priority, use a privately run luxury bus; tel: (0141) 511 6031 or 510 8370. Alwar, Sanganer, Sariska and Ranthambhore are well connected with Jaipur and each other by bus and **railway** networks. Make railway bookings at least a day in advance at the main station near Station Road; rail information tel: 131, reservations 135. When visiting Samode, travel by car or bus.

Ranthambhore and Sariska game-viewing tours are only possible in a pre booked jeep or truck, run by the National Parks; door-to-door pickup service. Otherwise, for Alwar and Sanganer, taxis or rickshaws are useful if walking proves too much. If travelling by train, take a taxi to your hotel.

Overnight stops are recommended in Ranthambhore, Samode and Sariska.

LUXURY

Sawai Madhopur Lodge, Ranthambhore National Park Road, Sawai Madhopur, tel: (07462) 220 541; www.tajhotels.com Former hunting lodge of Man Singh II, now a luxurious hotel with splendid gardens, restaurant, bar and pool. Also expensive tents.
Vanyavilas, Ranthambhore Road, Sawai Madhopur, tel: (07462) 223 999; e-mail: gm@oberoi-vanyavilas.com Luxurious air-conditioned tented rooms with private gardens and sundecks surround a building designed as a sumptuous royal hunting lodge, all set amongst lush gardens, with a pool, spa and lake.
Samode Palace-Hotel, Samode, Jaipur, tel: (0141) 263 2370, www.samode.com Regularly listed amongst the world's finest heritage hotels. Candle-lit verandah dinners, sumptuous Raj murals and furniture (see page 87). Pool, spa, cultural performances.
Sariska Palace, Sariska District, tel: (0144) 284 1322, Sariska@del2.vsnl.net.in www.sariska.com Former maharaja's palace, modestly dubbed 'lodge' by him. Opposite park entrance. Has a pool, gym, yoga centre, lovely garden, beautiful furnishings and verandahs.

MID-RANGE/BUDGET

Ankur Resort, Ranthambhore Road, tel: (07462) 220 792, fax: (07462) 223 303. Set in a garden, good value for clean rooms and reasonable food.
Hotel Tiger Safari Resort, Ranthambhore Road, tel: (07462) 221 137, deepak@tigersafariresort.com Pleasant hotel with a rooftop restaurant, rooms with wall paintings and some separate cottages.

Elephant Festival: Every year on the auspicious occasion of Holi (the festival of colours) in the month of March or April, dozens of elephants parade at the Chaugan stadium. **Gangaur Festival:** A festival in honour of Goddess Gauri in March/April near Holi. The Goddess is carried through the city, which is a big tourist attraction. **Teej Festival:** A celebration held in July/August to welcome the rains, eagerly awaited in the desert capital. **Jaipur Festival:** Takes place in November to revive old customs and traditions of princely Jaipur. **Kite Festival:** Takes place on 14 January and includes a Kite Fighting Competition and Display Flying.

Ranthambhore Tourist Information, RTDC Vinayak Tourist Complex, Ranthambhore Road; tel: (07462) 220 808. Open Mon–Sat 10:00–13:00, 13:30–17:00.
Project Tiger, Ranthambhore Road, Sawai Madhopur; http://projecttiger.nic.in

5
Agra

Today, the earliest Mughal garden, the Ram Bagh, is dry but you can still see the symmetrical design and the fruit trees, cypresses and poplars that Babur, and later his great-grandson Jahangir, planted. There are pavilions and perfect geometrical pools and terraces.

THE MUGHALS

The Mughals hailed from central Asia and had Turkish and Mongol blood in their veins. Babur, the founder of the empire of the Mughals in north India, was the ruler of the tiny central Asian kingdom of **Ferghanain**. He was a military adventurer who looked towards India for its wealth. In **1526** he defeated **Ibrahim Lodi**, the last of the Lodi sultans to rule north India at the famous **Battle of Panipat**. He then established Mughal control from **Kabul** to **Delhi** and **Agra**. Babur made Agra his capital, but his son **Humayun** moved to Delhi for a few years where he built his own city called **Dinpanah Akbar**, Humayun's son, returned to Agra. The city was at its most powerful in the 16th and 17th centuries. In 1648, Akbar's grandson **Shah Jahan** relocated to Delhi where he built **Shahjahanabad**, and from this time Agra began to decline. It was finally conquered by the **Jats** (a prosperous rural community who live in north India) in 1761 and by the British in 1803.

After Babur died, his son Humayun inherited the Mughal throne. Humayun was also a valiant soldier but Mughal power had still not been consolidated and he spent most of his short reign in battle with the rulers of Gujarat and with Afghan chieftains like **Sher Shah**.

DON'T MISS

*** Agra Fort: the seat of Mughal power during the 16th and 17th centuries.
*** The Taj Mahal: included in the list of the world's seven wonders. A must-see, especially at dusk or dawn.
*** Old City: stroll through the Old City in Agra and see artisans busy at work.
** Itimad-ud-Daulah's Tomb: visit this lovely tomb situated on the east bank of the Jamuna River.

Opposite: *The Taj Mahal, one of the world's greatest architectural wonders.*

PIETRA DURA

Pietra dura, a technique borrowed from Florence, is the name given to the **floral patterns** that the Mughals used to decorate their luxuriant architecture. They were lovers of nature, particularly gardens and flowers. *Pietra dura* became a special feature of Indo-Islamic architecture; the characteristic flowers and fruit motifs are not normally associated with Islamic buildings. *Pietra dura* is created from coloured stones such as marble, yellow, red and grey sandstone, lapis lazuli, as well as black slate. Tulips, lilies, irises and poppies were delicately inlaid in spray and arabesque patterns on a white marble background. This produced a richly ornamental look best exemplified in the Taj Mahal. Under torchlight, the stones glow with deep colour. *Pietra dura* work continues to be created by the descendants of the Taj Mahal craftsmen, and is nowadays also used to decorate contemporary items.

Humayun was deposed by Sher Shah in 1540, but won Delhi and Agra back in 1555.

It was Babur's grandson Akbar who took the Mughal empire to its greatest heights. '*The eyes are small but extremely vivid ... reveal a sharpness of mind and a keenness of intellect,*' wrote **Father Monserrate**, a visiting Jesuit missionary, about Akbar in 1580. Akbar conquered Rajputana in the west and parts of Bengal in the east, the Deccan in the south and Kashmir in the north. He created enormous prestige for the Mughal crown and developed efficient administrative systems like the *mansabdari* practice by which potentially rebellious Rajput and Afghan nobles were co-opted into the Mughal government. He realized the importance of integration and although a Muslim, married a Rajput princess, **Jodhai Bai** with whom he had his first son, **Jahangir**. He created a new religion – the *Din-i-Ilahi,* or *Sulh-i-Kul* (Peace to All) – in which all sectarian divisions were to be disregarded in supreme duty to a single god and emperor.

Akbar's son, **Jahangir**, who became emperor in 1605, was an equally able ruler, although addicted to drink and opium. His celebrated romance with a beautiful courtesan named **Anarkali**, is the stuff of legends and famous Bollywood films. During Jahangir's reign, the Mughal state became a lavish patron of the arts. Portraiture, music and architecture flourished under Jahangir. The

great artist **Mansur** painted the famous Mughal miniature birds at this time. Jahangir's most beautiful and powerful wife **Nur Jahan** built Agra's **Itimad-ud-Daulah** tomb, an extravagantly decorated structure, for her father. At this time, **Sir Thomas Roe**, envoy of James I, received a royal letter from

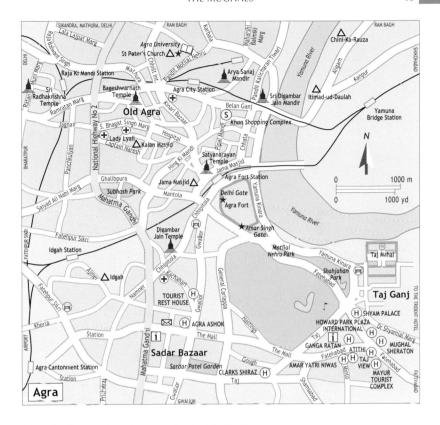

Agra

Jahangir allowing trade between the **East India Company** and India.

Jahangir was succeeded by his son **Shah Jahan**, the great builder who ensured the architectural glory of Mughals. Shah Jahan built the Red Fort in Delhi and, of course, the Taj Mahal – a mausoleum for his beloved wife **Mumtaz Mahal**. By the time Shah Jahan's son **Aurangzeb** came to the throne, the Mughal empire was over-extended and beginning to crumble under its own weight. Aurangzeb, the last great Mughal, was a controversial emperor. After Aurangzeb, the rulers who succeeded Aurangzeb were unable to maintain the empire in the face of threats from the Marathas, and later the British. They

Opposite: *Agra Fort, the Mughals' seat of power in the 16th and 17th centuries.*

Above: *Exterior of Amar Singh Gate.*

were further weakened by infighting and decadent living. The last Mughal, **Bahadur Shah Zafar** was deposed and exiled to **Burma** by the British where he died in 1862.

AGRA FORT

The first building at this site was called **Badalgarh** and was probably built by a Rajput ruler called Badal Singh. Later the Lodis built a fort here, which had fallen to ruin by the time Akbar commissioned his fort. Situated on the banks of the Yamuna River, this massive red sandstone structure was the seat of Mughal power during the reigns of three of the greatest Mughals – Akbar, his son Jahangir and grandson Shah Jahan. It was built by Akbar, extended by Jahangir and completed by Shah Jahan. The complete range of Mughal architectural styles can be seen in the fort, from military toughness to artistic embellishment. There are heavy sandstone walls, battlements and great gates, as well as delicate marble pavilions, marble basins, decorated walls and the characteristic *jaali* work.

Under Akbar's rule the fort was primarily a military stronghold with formidable walls and battlements. Jahangir gave it its perfumed fountains and ornamental baths. Shah Jahan added his imprimatur by adding white marble pillars and arches. Besides being the royal residence, Agra fort throbbed with military power. The grand ramparts enclosed an army well supplied with food and artillery. A moat runs along the outer and inner walls and the huge towers were designed for attacking approaching enemies. Agra Fort is a poignant building. It was here that emperor Aurangzeb imprisoned his father Shah Jahan, leaving the old man to gaze upon his beloved Taj Mahal from the Jasmine Tower as he slowly died.

The main entrance to the Fort, reached across the drawbridge, is through the huge **Amar Singh Gate**. In the first quadrangle, you will see the huge stone bath directly

TOURIST SCAMS

Agra is known for all kinds of clever methods to rip-off unsuspecting tourists, so be on guard. These scams range from minor annoyances like selling soapstone models of the Taj at vastly inflated prices to nasty ones like serving food designed to induce diarrhoea, then charging for medicines and doctors. Never accept food and drink unless you have made absolutely sure of the hotel and proprietor. There are rickshaw pullers who will put you down before the designated stop, fake ticket checkers who might take your ticket so you'll have to buy another and vendors and salesmen in the Taj Ganj area, opposite the Taj Mahal who grossly overcharge for their postcards and handicrafts. Always ensure that those who offer themselves as guides are properly authorized. In Agra, it is best to be as self sufficient as possible and not turn to anyone offering unsolicited help.

in front of Akbar's palaces. This bath was probably used by Jahangir's wife Nur Jahan, who, it is said, bathed in water scented with rose petals and is credited with inventing the sickly sweet Mughal perfume known as *attar*. The **Jahangir Mahal** which Akbar built for his first wife Jodhai Bai, mother of Jahangir and princess of the Rajput state of Amber, shows a combination of Islamic and Hindu styles. The palace is richly carved with floral patterns, birds and intricate arabesques. Blue-and-gold stucco paintings also decorate the walls. On the riverfront, there is a long open pavilion, in fact, the main verandah of the Jahangir Mahal, where the breezes coming from the river have a cooling effect; it provides a beautiful view of the opposite bank. Akbar is said to have lived in the Jahangir Mahal when he was not away on military campaigns. There are rooms for his harem, his library and his own living quarters.

Other, equally richly decorated palaces lie near the Jahangir Mahal: **Khas Mahal** (Unique Palace) and **Sheesh Mahal** (Mirror Palace), built as imperial lodgings. These are spacious and richly decorated with niches for lamps and with enclosed doorways. Khas Mahal was known as Shah Jahan's *aram garh* or relaxation room. Outside the Khas Mahal is the **Anguri Bagh** or grape garden that is surrounded with rooms for court women. The Mughals were from central Asia and unused to the heat of the Indian plains. Deep darkened rooms, interspersed with fountains, were designed for coolness and to provide maximum protection from the sun's glare.

The **Musamman Burj** or **Jasmine Tower** has been described as a palace 'hanging like a fairy bower over the grim ramparts'. Its central room has a marble basin and a giant fountain, its walls are covered in *pietra dura* and *jaalis* and set with niches for lamps and vases. It was a grim irony that this fabulous palace, built by Shah Jahan, would one day become his prison, where he would live out the last of his days tended by his devoted daughter Jahanara.

AMAR SINGH'S LEAP

The main gate of Agra Fort is Amar Singh Gate, named after a Rajput nobleman at the court of emperor Shah Jahan. Amar Singh committed an unpardonable error by slaying the royal treasurer for having slighted him in front of the emperor. Distraught at his own recklessness he rode his horse over the fort walls. The horse died and the hot-blooded Rajput was executed, but Shah Jahan was so impressed by this dramatic act that he named the main gate of the palace after him.

Below: *Red stone carving being restored.*

Taj Mahal

THE TAJ IN LITERATURE

The exquisite and melancholic beauty of the Taj Mahal has been written about by visitors through the ages. **Rabindranath Tagore** described it as 'a tear on the face of eternity'. Colonel JA Hodgson, Surveyor General of India wrote in the 19th century: 'From the temptation to liken it to a fairy fabric built of pearl or moonlight, those who intend to visit the Taj are apt to form an idea that though beautiful, it is small; it is of considerable dimensions and altitude ... It is, I suppose, one of the most perfect and beautiful buildings in the world.' **Eleanor Roosevelt**, when she first saw it said: 'I held my breath, unable to speak in the face of so much beauty. I wanted to drink in its beauty from a distance ... this is a beauty that enters the soul. With its minarets rising at each corner, its dome and tapering spires, it creates a sense of airy almost floating lightness. I had never known what perfect proportions were before'.

The **Diwan-i-Am** (Hall of the People) and **Diwan-i-Khas** (Hall of the Noblemen) are built on a grand scale, again decorated with columns and carved walls. The emperor heard grievances of the people in the colonnaded Diwan-i-Am, seated on his famous **Peacock Throne**, which is said to have been set with rubies, diamonds and other precious stones. The Diwan-i-Khas – overlooking a long riverside verandah and situated on the terrace above the Mussaman Burj a floor above the Diwan-i-Am – was reserved for important guests. There are two thrones at the Diwan-i-Khas, one white and one black. The latter was created specially for Jahangir when he became emperor after a long wait and several rebellions against his father, at the age of 35.

Don't miss the **Machchi Bhavan** or Fish House, a large sunken fish pond with surrounding harem quarters. Meena Bazaar, situated at the northern side of the fort, was a market offering handicrafts and precious stones, and a lively evening spot for the inhabitants of the mosque, where the emperors flirted with courtesans. It was here that Jahangir met his **Nur Jahan** and Shah Jahan his **Mumtaz Mahal**.

The **Moti Masjid** (Pearl Mosque), built by Shah Jahan, is a blindingly white marble mosque located deep within the rooms of the Fort. It was a private place of worship for the nobility. Open daily, sunrise to sunset.

THE TAJ MAHAL

For first time visitors and the local traveller, it's impossible not to be struck by the ethereal sad beauty of the Taj Mahal. The most cynical of world travellers have been silenced by this stunning structure that is almost vulnerable in its purity. The elegant white marble, slim minarets and floating dome create a sense of untouched romance, 'the proud passion of an emperor's love', as **Edwin Arnold** enthused. Of course, Shah Jahan would have been horrified at the pollution levels of modern Agra, a city now classified by the World Health Organization as 'pollution intensive zone'. With sections of the Taj's white marble becoming discoloured and brittle, experts have been giving it an ayurvedic face pack of fuller's earth, cereal, milk and lime, with spectacular results. Over 200 industries have been ordered to move out of this area, and cars, buses and scooters are banned within a 500m (1641 feet) radius of the Taj, but Agra remains a highly congested and polluted city and the fumes may one day take their toll on this most beautiful of India's buildings. For the moment, however, it certainly appears as dazzling as it has always been, well worth more than one single visit.

The love story of the emperor Shah Jahan and Mumtaz Mahal is well known throughout India. Shah Jahan, or Prince Khurram, as he was known before he ascended the throne, fell madly in love with the beautiful Arjumand Banu Begum, married her and gave her the title Mumtaz Mahal (Exalted one of the Palace). When she died in 1631 while giving birth to her 14th child, the emperor was so distraught that he mourned her death for two years, his hair turned grey overnight and he even stopped eating meat or listening to music. Quite a sacrifice for the high living Mughals! He promised to build the most beautiful mausoleum ever known to the world. After it was commissioned, the Taj took 22 years to build. It cost nearly 400 million rupees, used 500kg (1103 pounds) of gold, and approximately 20,000 men and women toiled on it. All the marble was imported from Rajasthan, turquoise from Persia and diamonds from central Asia. The names of the architects are unknown. Some sources say that the chief architect was one **Ustad Ahmad Lahori**, others say it was

UNHAPPY FAMILIES

Architecture and military glory aside, the Mughals have gone down in history as a succession of big, unhappy families. But no Mughal could compete with the grim, fanatical Aurangzeb who managed to eliminate all the males in his family in an effort to obtain and keep his throne. First, he incarcerated his younger brother Murad who was an opium addict. His elder brother, and favourite of Shah Jahan and the people, Darah Sukoh, was mercilessly pursued, put to death, and his head presented to their heartbroken father. Aurangzeb also ordered the imprisonment and execution of Darah Sukoh's handsome son at Gwalior Fort. He finally removed his own father from the throne and imprisoned him at Agra Fort, where the great Shah Jahan spent his last years gazing disconsolately at the distant Taj Mahal that contained the remains of his beloved Mumtaz. Critics blame Aurangzeb for his religious intolerance which, after centuries of harmony, spelt the beginning of the end for the Mughal empire.

Left: *Entrance gateway to the Taj Mahal.*

SHOPPING

The Old City is a good place
for handicrafts. Gangotri in
the Taj Mahal Complex is a
state run emporium and stocks
fabric, shoes and *objets d'art*.
Miniature Taj Mahals in ivory
(illegal to take home), glass,
soapstone, wax, and bamboo
are all available in the Taj
Ganj area. Watch out here for
aggressive sales and high
prices. Koh-i-Noor on the
Mahatma Gandhi Road stocks
traditional jewellery. There are
a number of textile shops here
too, offering the fine soft
cotton cloth known as *mal
mal*, and the printed cotton
known as 'bizzie lizzie'. The
shopping arcade at the Mughal
Sheraton is very well stocked
but expensive. **Fabrics**, jackets
and caps embroidered in the
zardozi (gold embroidery) style
are sold in Old Agra. For a
selection of **shoe shops**, Sadar
Bazaar is the best. Marble
inlay work and *pietra dura* can
be found throughout the city.
Also look at the local **carpets**;
this is where the Mughal
Imperial carpets were made
and you could take home a
traditional design. Other temp-
tations include spices and
miniature paintings. Most of
the large emporia and set-price
shops line Fatehabad Road.
Prices for textiles and jewellery
are generally cheaper in Jaipur.

Persian **Isa Khan**. Designers were brought in from overseas
– Mohammad Afandi from Turkey, Mullah Mushid from
Persia and Geronimo Veroneo, whose grave can be found
in the Roman Catholic cemetery in Agra, from Venice.

The original entrance to the Taj was a huge red sandstone arch which housed a market complex. You cannot
enter through this gate anymore, but by a small door to the
right where you are frisked by security guards. The gateway is inscribed with verses from the 89th chapter of
the Qur'an, one of which reads: '*So enter as one of his
servants, and enter into his garden.*'

The Taj was built to resemble paradise on earth and the
doors of the gateway were apparently once made of solid
silver that was later plundered by invading tribes of **Jats**.
As you enter, you see the first picture postcard view of the
Taj, floating above the ground, its great dome deceptively
near. The garden, divided into eight squares in the
charbagh style is laid out along the central waterway in
front of the mausoleum. Rows of cypresses line this long
canal and the lotus pool, named after the lotus-shaped
fountain spouts. The perfectly symmetrical reflection of the
Taj in the water of the lotus pool emphasizes the marvel of
its architecture.

The Taj stands on a marble platform about 8m (22
feet) high and covering an area of 95m² (313 square feet).
Since you cannot see the platform from the gateway, it

Right: *Replicas of the
cenotaphs of Mumtaz
Mahal and Shah Jahan.*

looks as if the mausoleum is floating. Up close, the staggering detail of the carvings, *pietra dura* lilies and tulips, Qur'anic inscriptions, inlaid precious and semi-precious stones – most of them vandalized and gouged out by now – show the care and attention that the artisans lavished on this building. Four small domes surround the central dome of the Taj. Directly below the central dome in the octagonal burial chamber lie the false cenotaphs of Mumtaz Mahal and Shah Jahan. The real ones are housed in a basement directly beneath. The burial chamber is lit by daylight filtering through marble *jaalis* and is superbly decorated with *pietra dura* and **Qur'anic** inscriptions. It has been said that the only discordant note in the Taj is, ironically enough, the tomb of Shah Jahan which his son Aurangzeb placed next to that of Mumtaz. The building was designed so that Mumtaz's tomb would be its single centrepiece under the central dome – Shah Jahan's tomb breaks the pattern.

Above: *The Taj Mahal with local children in the foreground near the Mehtab Bagh.*

On either side of the Taj stand two sandstone edifices – a mosque and what was probably a royal guesthouse. The mosque is impressive, but pales in comparison to the Taj.

Some say that Shah Jahan planned a black Taj on the opposite bank of the Yamuna, but there is no evidence that construction was ever begun on such a structure.

Sunrise and sunset are the best times to visit the Taj Mahal. The marble catches and reflects the light in such a manner that it would seem as though the architects and designers were seeking some sort of union with the sun and moon, so that their creation would complement the movements of the heavenly bodies. The Taj has been described as the Islamic concept of paradise.

Across the river from the Taj, a Mughal garden, the **Mehtab Bagh**, is being restored. It's a wonderful place from which to watch the sunset, with superb views of the Taj.

ENTRY TO THE TAJ

The Taj is open 06:00–19:00 every day except Monday. At the time of writing, the ticket is Rs750 for foreigners, but this gives a discount at all other Agra monuments visited on the same day. For five days a month, surrounding the full moon, the Taj opens from 20:30 to 00:30. Tickets are only available in advance from the Archaeology Survey of India (see page 105). The Taj museum is open every day except Monday and Friday and entry is free. It contains lithographs of the Taj, old photographs and information on the materials used in the construction.

Above: *A craftsman fashions a table using the* pietra dura *technique.*
Opposite: *Inside, Agra Fort is really a city within a city.*

THE OLD CITY

At the time of Jahangir and Shah Jahan, Agra was one of the great cities in the world, famous for its commercial activity and military strength. As traveller Ralph Fitch wrote in 1584, '*Agra is a very great citie and populous … it hath a faire castle … either one of them (Agra and Fatehpur Sikri) much greater than London.*' During the reign of the Mughals, Agra was crowded and rich, with schools, bazaars, *hammams* (baths) and magnificent royal buildings. Walking around the Old City of Agra, one can see remains of this past here and there, but generally it is a crazily crowded area, congested with cows, cycle-rickshaws and ubiquitous Maruti cars edging through heaps of vegetables and flowers lying in open stalls along the road.

Shopping in Agra

All sorts of merchandise can be found here, from dried fruit to walking sticks, kites and sweets. The Old City is a maze of narrow alleyways and it is very easy to get lost. The latest Bollywood songs blare out from shop fronts and directly opposite these are businesses selling washing machines and irons. Highly skilled craftsmen, working with dedication at their marble inlay work or *zardozi* (fabrics embroidered with gold or silver thread), line the streets. Descendants of the old master craftsmen still live among the ruined *havelis* and above the narrow streets. Kinari Bazaar is a good shopping area here, but watch out for overpriced poor-quality products. *Dhurries* are the speciality of Agra and the best shops are in the Old City in Johri Bazaar. Other Agra specialities are leather shoes, *gajak* (a sweet) and the famous *zardozi*. There are a number of jewellery shops and good *zardozi* work in **Kinari Bazaar**. Many Henna artists line the bazaar; you can get a temporary tattoo done for about 150 rupees per hand; patterns range from the traditional to the bizarre. Other markets include the **Loha Mandi** (iron market) and **Sabzi Mandi** (vegetable market). **Nai ki Mandi**, north of the Jama Masjid is the best place to find traditional leather shoes as well as *pietra dura* craftsmen. The work is slow and laborious and a small box can take up to a month to complete. The best place to find excellent *pietra dura* handicrafts is **Subhash Emporium** on Gwalior Road where they even have a book that contains specific *pietra dura* details of the Taj and can recreate them on demand.

Jama Masjid

At the centre of old Agra, surrounded by clamorous markets, stands the **Jama Masjid** which Shah Jahan built for his eldest, most accomplished and favourite daughter **Jahanara**. This is Agra's busiest mosque and is jampacked on Fridays. Unlike other mosques four corners of the the Jama Masjid are not accented by tall minarets, but its dome is decorated with an eyecatching red sandstone and a white marble zig-zag pattern. Possibly because the mosque has been maintained by princesses, it has a special chamber reserved for women, and the water tank features a *shahi chirag* (royal stove) for heating water.

AGRA CANTONMENT

Also known as Agra Cantt, it was built by the British in the 19th century. This area is typically British Raj with its wide avenues and now rather dilapidated bungalows. As you travel down Mall Road, it is easy to imagine colonial officials cycling to **Queen Mary's Library** or **St**

> ### LIGHT OF THE WORLD
>
> Itimad-ud-Daulah's tomb, known as the 'baby Taj' among rickshaw drivers, was built by Nur Jahan, Jahangir's queen and the most influential woman in the history of the Mughals. Nur Jahan wanted to make her father's tomb entirely of silver, but was warned that it would be disassembled by looters. Nur Jahan (light of the world, a name given to her by the adoring Jahangir), was so powerful that coins were minted in her image, and her father Ghiyas Beg, although of humble origins, was promoted to imperial minister and named Itimad-ud-Daulah (Lord Treasurer).

George's Church. Sadly, most of the cantonment buildings have been allowed to fall into disrepair, although some of them continue to be occupied by public offices and departments. St George's Church, designed by the architect JT Boileau, is a long building with a four storeyed tower, built in the familiar style of other churches in North India. **St John's College** is also worth a visit. It is regarded as one of the best educational institutions in North India and was built of red sandstone in imitation Fatehpur Sikri-style by Samuel Swinton Jacob.

Ram Bagh

Across the Yamuna River, on the opposite bank of the Taj Mahal, you find the **Ram Bagh** (also Rambagh Garden of Rest and Paradise Garden). This first Mughal garden was created by Babur and laid out according to the *charbag* principles.

Being used to the cool greens of Persia, Babur was disappointed by the dry heat of India and wrote: '*One of the great defects of Hindustan is its lack of running waters, it kept coming to my mind that water should be made to flow by means of wheels wherever I might settle down, also that grounds should be laid out in an orderly and symmetrical form.*' He tried to recreate a similar landscape on the Indian plain. At Ram Bagh, the waterways intersect at a central point where a pavilion was built for the emperor. A complicated system of underground wells was dug to keep up a constant flow of water to the garden from the Yamuna. The garden is now just a shadow of its former self, the grass is parched and the fountains have run dry, but you can still admire the picturesque *charbagh* design.

Opposite: *Itimad-ud-Daulah's tomb, built by his daughter Nur Jahan.*
Below: *Veiled Rajasthani women at the Taj Mahal.*

ITIMAD-UD-DAULAH'S TOMB

South from the Ram Bagh is the tomb of Itimad-ud-Daulah that has been described as a 'jewel box of marble'. It was built by Jahangir's queen, Nur Jahan for her father, Ghiyas Beg, a soldier of fortune who rose to prominence in Akbar's time and was given the title Itimad-ud-Daulah (Lord Treasurer) by Jahangir. Historians

have written that Nur Jahan had this tomb built in the grandest possible manner because she was anxious to affect a high monarchical style to hide her humble origins. A small structure, the tomb is astounding in the wealth of its carvings, mosaic, lattice and inlay work. It marks the transition from the no-nonsense red sandstone architecture of Akbar to the more refined, sensuous and delicate ornamentation of Jahangir and Shah Jahan. The flasks of wine patterned on the walls of the tomb have been interpreted as Nur Jahan's private joke on her alcoholic husband. They are a significant departure from Islamic architecture in which representations of wine are prohibited.

CHINI-KA-RAUZA

North from Itimad-ud-Daulah, also overlooking the river, is the tomb of **Afzal Khan** known as **Chini-ka-Rauza** (China Tomb). Afzal Khan was a Persian scholar and important nobleman during the reign of Shah Jahan. This tomb was once covered with green and blue glazed tiles and decorated with verses from the Qur'an as well as the *pietra dura* patterns. Virtually nothing remains of the tiled façade, but the burial chamber still provides glimpses of the ornamental plaster patterns which were used to decorate tombs at this time.

CHARBAGH

All the Mughal emperors loved gardens, so much so that the term Mughal Garden has entered the lexicon of Indian architecture to describe a geometrically planned lush area of land, decorated with pavilions and pools. *Char* means four, *bagh* means garden. *Charbagh* therefore indicates a garden plan that is divided into four squares (supposed to represent the four periods of life – childhood, adolescence, middle age and old age) by the axis of the central water canal. The first Mughal garden, created in Agra by Babur, was called the **Ram Bagh** or **Rambagh** and the *charbagh* principle was used in almost all Mughal tombs, including Humayun's in Delhi later copied by British architect Edwin Lutyens when he designed the viceroy's house in New Delhi, now the presidential residence.

Agra at a Glance

BEST TIMES TO VISIT

Oct–Mar is the best time to visit Agra. Minimum temperatures range from 19°C (66°F) to 8°C (46°F). Maximum temperatures are 35°C (95°F) to 23°C (73°F). By mid-Sep, the monsoon generally peters out across northern India. The weather in the Golden Triangle is cool and dry from Oct–Mar but winter mornings can be foggy and very cold. **Jan** can turn smoggy and chilly, and light rainfall is not uncommon.

GETTING THERE

Agra is 204km (127 miles) from Delhi, with good road and rail links. Train 2002 (**Bhopal Shatabdi**) departs New Delhi 06:15, arrives Agra 08:12; train 2616 (**GT Express**) departs New Delhi 18:40, arrives Agra 21:45; train 2001 (**NDLS Shatabdi E**) departs Agra 20:30, arrives New Delhi 22:30; see also www.indianrail.gov.in **Indian Airlines** runs a daily air shuttle service from Delhi to Varanasi and Khajuraho via Agra. Buses from Delhi to Agra leave from the Inter State Bus Terminus. Luxury coaches take 90 min and terminate at Idgah bus stand at Agra. Buses are crowded so it's best to use the train or the air service. Agra's **Kheria Airport** is 7km (4 miles) from town. Use a prepaid taxi at the airport or station rather than risk being overcharged. Book coaches, trains or airlines through travel agents. Hiring a car and driver for the day or for

several days can be cheap, especially if costs are shared. **Jet Air**, Hotel Clarks Shiraz, Taj Road, tel: (0562) 222 6521-3. **Indian Airlines**, Clarks Shiraz, tel: (0562) 222 6821. **Airport information**, tel: (0562) 240 0569. **Train information**, tel: 131 (computer enquiry system); (0562) 242 1039 (Cantt).

GETTING AROUND

Cycle-rickshaws and prepaid taxis are the best way to get around, or arrange on arrival a rate for the full day. Do this from the hotel or via the tourist office to ensure a fair rate. Haji Tours and Travels, 435 Sultanpura, mobile: 9837 253 172, is a reliable source of fixed price taxis and can also provide government approved guides.

WHERE TO STAY

LUXURY

ITC Mughal, Agra, Taj Ganj, Agra, tel: (0562) 233 1701, fax: (0562) 233 1730. Luxurious hotel in Mughal style, near Taj Mahal. Enclosed courtyards and gardens on a huge property. Excellent service, pool, health centre, fine restaurants including north-west frontier Peshawari, the poolside Bagh-e-Bahar, Taj Bano buffet, Mah Jong Chinese room, a coffee shop and a cocktail bar. Plus a shopping mall.
Oberoi Amarvilâs, Taj East Gate Road, tel: (0562) 223 1515, gm@oberoi-

amarvilas.com Like a Mughal fort in its glory days, this hotel was built in traditional Mughal style, with every luxury.
Hotel Yamuna View, 6B The Mall, tel: (0562) 246 2990, sales@hotelyamunaviewagra.com A privatized hotel, clean but with a slightly municipal character. Large, comfortable rooms, courteous staff. Pool.
Howard Park Plaza International, Fatehabad Road, tel: (0562) 400 1870-4, hpp@sarovarhotels.com A bit kitsch but very clean, with tip-top maintenance and an excellent poolside restaurant service.
Clarks Shiraz, 54 Taj Road, tel: (0562) 222 6121, info@hotelclarksshiraz.com India's first five-star hotel and one of Agra's oldest, now definitely overtaken by the opposition. The rooms are tired but have lovely views of the Taj Mahal; the food is adequate rather than good. Pool. Central with many useful offices and agencies on the premises.

MID-RANGE

Hotel Mansingh Palace, Fatehabad Road, tel: (0562) 233 1771, sales.agra@mansinghhotels.com Red sandstone building with lots of architectural details; airy, recently renovated rooms.
Grand, 137 Station Road, Agra Cantt, tel: (0562) 222 7514, fax: (0562) 364 271.
Hotel Atithi, Fatehabad Road, tel: (0562) 233 0878, e-mail: hotelatithi@hotmail.com

Amar Yatri Niwas, Fatehabad Rd, tel: (0562) 223 3030, fax: (0562) 223 3035, reservation@ amaryatriniwas.com
Ganga Ratan, Fatehabad Rd, tel: (0562) 223 2660-3, info@hotelgangaratan.com

BUDGET

Most of the budget hotels are in Taj Ganj, a bustling area behind the Taj Mahal. There are plenty of cheap restaurants and hotels here, although this is the place where one needs to be on the look out for scams, pickpockets and hotel rip-offs. The hotels are generally clean, the staff are friendly and can be helpful with organizing tours.
Tourist Guest House, 4/62 Kutchery Road, Baluganj, Agra, tel: (0562) 246 3961, dontworrychickencurry@ hotmail.com www.dont worrychickencurry.com Quiet, comfortable guesthouse, with garden, terrace and rooftop vegetarian restaurant, plus internet facilities; owner will organize tours. The same owners run the **Hotel Satari**, Shamsabad Road, tel: (0562) 233 3029. Other budget hotels include:
Bawa Palace, Old Idgah Colony; tel: (0562) 242 0151.
Sheela Hotel, Eastern Gate, Taj Mahal, Agra, tel: (0562) 233 3074/1194, e-mail: hotel sheelaagraindia@yahoo.com

WHERE TO EAT

Agra is not well known for fine dining. For safe, good-quality food, it's best to eat at the five-star hotels. The restaurants and bar at the Mughal Sheraton are the best, particularly for northwest frontier cuisine at the Peshawari. The Trident and Clarks Shiraz are good for sandwiches and kebabs.

Dasaprakash, Balu Ganj, off Gwalior Road, part of the all-Indian chain of Dasaprakash restaurants, provides the usual South Indian fare of *dosas*, *idlis* and South Indian coffee.
Zorba the Buddha, Osho Restaurant, off Gwalior Road, is run by the followers of the Rajneesh or Osho spiritual college. Vegetarian, very clean.

Only Restaurant, Mall Road, is typical of the eateries found in mid-sized towns of North India, offering wholesome, unpretentious meals. Garden tables. In the evenings, there is live Indian music.

TOURS AND EXCURSIONS

The **UP State Tourism Development Corporation** offers daily tours of the Taj Mahal, Agra Fort and Fatehpur Sikri (10:15–18:15). Bookings through the tourist offices (*see* below). Local travel agents also offer a range of tours to Fatehpur Sikri, Bharatpur and Deeg, Sikandra, Mathura and Gwalior.
TCI Travel Agency, Hotel Clarks Shiraz; tel: (0562) 222 6521-3, tciagra@tci.co.in
UP Tourism office, 64 Taj Road, tel: (0562) 222 6431; agratourism@gmail.com
Cantt Railway Station, Agra, tel: (0562) 242 0998.
Government of India Tourist office, 191 The Mall, tel: (0562) 222 6368/78
There are plenty of ATMs that accept foreign cards, if you need to change money.

USEFUL CONTACTS

District Hospital, Mahatma Gandhi Rd, tel: (0562) 246 3043, 226 2032, 226 3857.
Quick Silver Courier Service, Block 43, Sanjay Place 2, tel: (0562) 285 3389.
Blue Dart Express Ltd, Raman Tower, Sanjay Place, tel: (0562) 400 5106/8731.
Archaeological Survey, The Mall, tel: (0562) 222 7261
Police, tel: (0562) 236 3898, 226 2221, 226 0601, or just dial 100.

AGRA	J	F	M	A	M	J	J	A	S	O	N	D
AVERAGE TEMP. °C	14	17	23	29	34	35	31	30	30	27	21	16
AVERAGE TEMP. °F	57	63	73	84	93	95	88	86	86	81	70	61
HOURS SUN DAILY	11	12	12	12	14	14	14	14	13	12	12	11
RAINFALL mm	25	22	17	7	8	65	211	173	150	31	1	5
RAINFALL in	1	0.9	0.7	0.3	0.3	2.5	8.2	6.8	5.9	1.2	0.04	0.2

6
Around Agra

Only a small detour to the west of Agra will take you to the stunning ghost city of **Fatehpur Sikri**, once a seat of the Mughal empire under the free-thinking emperor Akbar. Even after seeing the Taj Mahal, this haunted city does not fail to impress. The **Keoladeo Ghana National Park** in Bharatpur, approximately 55km (34 miles) from Agra, is a must see for bird lovers, with over 300 species. The Water Palace in sleepy **Deeg** illustrates monsoon architecture beautifully. Landmarks **Mathura** and **Vrindavan** are famous for their connection with Lord Krishna and for being busy sites of Hindu worship and pilgrimage.

FATEHPUR SIKRI

If the Taj Mahal was Shah Jahan's signature and embodiment of the artistic and romantic aspects of his reign, then Fatehpur Sikri is Akbar's architectural autograph, built in his favourite red sandstone. Akbar was a tough empire builder and might have been impatient with the marble delicacies so favoured by his son and grandson. The buildings in Fatehpur Sikri are impressive and robust, but lack the finesse of later Mughal architecture. Akbar was engaged almost continuously in battles on all fronts to consolidate his empire. The architecture shows a fusion of the Islamic and Hindu styles. During the time that the city was being built Akbar was fighting with the rulers of Gujarat so several features of Gujarati architecture, such as the carved brackets in the Diwan-i-Khas (House of Private Audience), have been incorporated.

DON'T MISS

*** Fatehpur Sikri: Akbar's 'City of Victory'.
*** Keoladeo National Park: a world heritage site, home to over 300 species of birds.
*** Water Palace at Deeg: a breathtaking piece of Monsoon architecture (see page 113).
*** Mathura and Vrindavan: tour the temples and ghats in the holy Krishna sites.
*** Gwalior hilltop fort: the views are incredible.
*** Orchha: a ghost town off the beaten track.

Opposite: *Entrance gateway to the Jama Masjid i Fatehpur Sikri.*

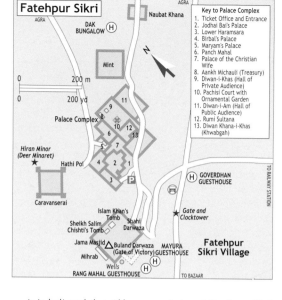

Fatehpur Sikri

Key to Palace Complex
1. Ticket Office and Entrance
2. Jodhai Bai's Palace
3. Lower Haramsara
4. Birbal's Palace
5. Maryam's Palace
6. Panch Mahal
7. Palace of the Christian Wife
8. Aankh Michauli (Treasury)
9. Diwan-i-Khas (Hall of Private Audience)
10. Pachisi Court with Ornamental Garden
11. Diwan-i-Am (Hall of Public Audience)
12. Rumi Sultana
13. Diwan Khana-i-Khas (Khwabgah)

AKBAR'S PRINCIPLES OF RELIGION

Akbar's foremost aim when he came to the throne was to integrate his huge multi-lingual, multi-religious unruly empire. In 1575 he built his **Ibadat Khana**, where he invited scholars from all religions to teach him what he called the 'principles of true religion.' Through these discussions he arrived at the set of beliefs known as the *Din-i-Ilahi* or the *Sulh-i-kul* (Peace to All). These beliefs asked followers to rise above sect and creed and follow a single God, whose representative was the emperor. This was an attempt by Akbar to create a notion of sovereignty by which people of diverse faiths and beliefs would be loyal to the king. According to *sulh-i-kul*, it was the duty of the ruler to treat all his subjects with ~aternal love, irrespective of ~ligion or ethnicity.

It is believed that Akbar commissioned Fatehpur Sikri after his son was born. He had waited for a male heir for many years and was overjoyed when his Rajput wife gave birth to Salim, later called Jahangir, in 1569, a year after his annual pilgrimage to the Sufi saints at Ajmer. He was anxious to create a monument to his rule and bolster the prestige of the Mughal throne. Located 37km (23 miles) west of Agra, Fatehpur Sikri was built in 1571 and was the capital of the Mughal empire for 14 years.

Nobody knows why Akbar suddenly abandoned it, perhaps water supplies ran out or he was called away on a military campaign (*see* page 110).

The main entrance to the city is through the **Buland Darwaza** (Gate of Victory) built to commemorate Akbar's victory in Gujarat. It stands 54m (177 feet) tall and makes a medieval diving board for young men from the neighbouring village.

A section of the city houses the private quarters of the emperor, consisting of the **Khwabgah** (House of Dreams) sleeping quarters that overlook a lake called Anoop Talao.

It is a colonnaded building that was cooled by the breeze blowing in from the water. The emperor's wives came to him through latticed passages connecting his quarters with the harem.

The Anoop Talao or peerless Pool, set in the middle of a square, has a platform at the centre where Tansen, the legendary court musician sat. He was apparently such an accomplished musician that he was able to light lamps and create rainfall whenever he wished, through the sheer power of his voice. In a corner of the square is the small but exquisite pavilion of the Turkish sultana, one of Akbar's favourite wives. It could have served as a *hammam* or even as an informal discussion chamber. The elaborate carvings of pomegranates, palms and fabulous animals betray mixed influences from Persia, Turkey and even China.

The public area consists of the treasury, the **Diwan-i-Am** (Hall of Public Audience) and the harem. Then there is the sacred area where the delicately carved marble tomb of saint Sheikh Salim Chishti (the only marble structure in the city) and the Jama Masjid stands. Another great gateway, decorated with characteristic *chhatris* (small pavilions), the **Badshahi Darwaza** separates the royal living quarters from the sacred area.

The largest open courtyard at Fatehpur Sikri is the **Pachisi Court**. This was apparently used as a giant chess board on which courtesans played the parts of chess pieces while the emperor watched and directed them from the overlooking Panch Mahal. The fantastic Panch Mahal is a large five-storeyed pavilion open to cool breezes on all sides. There are 176 columns, none of which are exactly the same and it has a

---

JODHAI BAI

By the age of 26, Akbar had assembled 300 wives and a harem of 5000 concubines and yet he had no heir. It was the Rajput princess, Jodhai Bai of Amber, who gave him his first son Salim, later to become the emperor Jahangir. To celebrate this event, Akbar ordered the construction of Fatehpur Sikri. He was so fond of Jodhai Bai that he shaved off his beard and stopped eating onions and garlic which, according to her, were 'inconvenient in kissing'. He also gave up beef so as not to offend her Hindu principles.

Below: *Emperor Akbar's Tomb in Sikandra 8km (5 miles) from Agra.*

Only 14 years after its construction, Fatehpur Sikri was
deserted forever. The entire
court, including 1000 door-
keepers and 1200 horses,
broke camp and abandoned
the city to wild animals. It is
not known what caused this
sudden departure. Water
shortage, military pressure on
the northwest border of the
kingdom, or the difficulty of
maintaining two palaces (one
each in Sikri and Agra), may
have been the reasons. In the
words of historian Richard
Lannoy, Sikri was *'a tragic
political failure'* but *'its failure
has nothing to do with its
architecture, which remains
the most perfect expression
of the liberal society which
Indian rulers have vainly
striven to realize.'*

superb view of the surrounding fields. In Akbar's time,
there must have been a view of the river. The steps are
rather steep and climbing them is certainly a calorie-
burning exercise but must have been very pleasant in the
evenings. The ladies of the harem sat out on the Panch
Mahal on summer nights with their emperor.

The Diwan-i-Am and Diwan-i-Khas are the two main
public halls of the city. The Diwan-i-Am is built like a
large open courtyard where the emperor held his public
hearings and occasional public prayers. This is also where
he married his queen.

The **Diwan-i-Khas** (Hall of Private Audience) is a richly
carved building, with interiors heavily influenced by
Hindu styles. The curving staircase and the carved cross
beams could easily pass for the interior of a Gujarati
palace. The giant carved capital at the building's centre
from which four walkways radiate towards a circular balcony, is a masterpiece. This is where Akbar sat on his

Opposite: *Akbar's unique
Diwan-i-Khas overlooking
the Pachisi Court.*
Right: *Sheikh Salim
Chishti's tomb attracts
crowds in search of a
miracle.*

throne and surveyed his domain. The two-storeyed façade of the Diwan-i-Khas is square and boxy, with *chhatris* at either ends of the roof.

Yet another important public building is the **Aankh Michauli**, the treasury which stands behind the Diwan-i-Khas. The strange name comes from the story that the emperor played hide and seek here with ladies of the harem. Stone monsters guard the building's dark interior where the royal gold and silver was stored.

The **Jama Masjid** in the southwest corner is a huge open structure, with *chhatris* on its roof, delicate *jaali* work at either end and an open verandah lined with carved pillars.

To the west, the women's quarters or *zenana* include the main harem, several separate residences for the queens as well as a royal garden. The imposing **Jodhai Bai's Palace**, named after Akbar's favourite wife, was guarded by eunuchs and is where the emperor reputedly spent his nights. There is a section which was democratically converted into a temple for the Hindu contingent of the harem. The fusion of decorative styles is remarkable: we find elements of Gujarat and Gwalior art such as the blue tile work on the ceiling, mixed with Islamic details. The beautiful tulip motif is the city's blueprint.

> ### TROUBLE IN THE FAMILY
>
> Akbar's long-awaited son Salim was somewhat of a disappointment at first. Biding his time in the opulence of the court, Salim succumbed to debauchery, betraying his father's high aspirations, while his two younger brothers drank themselves to death. Akbar turned his attention to his grandson as a potential heir to the throne, thus inciting the bitter Salim to murder his father's gifted protégé and biographer Abu'l Fazl. Akbar arranged a fight between the elephants of his sons Salim and Khusrau. Salim's elephant won and shortly afterwards, the wayward prince became a capable emperor: Jahangir, 'Seizer of the World'.

Across from Jodhai Bai's Palace, **Maryam's Palace** has obscure origins. It could have been named after a Christian queen, although there are no records to substantiate this claim. It is also possible that Akbar's mother lived here. The inside walls were once lined with gold frescoes depicting angels, birds and animals, hence the other name of the residence – **Sunhera Makan** (Golden House). There was an inscription on the wall once penned by Abu'l Fazl, the royal biographer: 'The gardens painted on these walls are on a par with the gardens of paradise'.

It is a mystery why the third and finest main building of the zenana, **Birbal's Palace**, was named after Akbar's trusted advisor who could not have lived in the women's quarters. Birbal the Wise, the musician Tansen and the biographer Abu'l Fazl were three of the 'Nine Gems' at Akbar's court. This residence has preserved its intricate stone carvings of lotus blossoms and geometric forms.

Fatehpur Sikri is a ghost city today but at sunset when a red glow illuminates the ruins, you can imagine the life of the young and vigorous king: his harem, his debate hall, houses for his wives and mistresses, his mosque, the public buildings and the giant courtyard for his live chess games. Rich carpets and curtains adorned the palace, water flowed in its gardens and rose bushes lined the pools. Outside the city on the banks of the river Akbar is said to have played polo and watched his favourite sport: elephant fights.

MAKING A WISH AT CHISHTI'S TOMB

The tomb of the Sufi saint, Sheikh Salim Chishti, is an exquisitely carved marble structure inside Fatehpur Sikri. Legend has it that only after Salim Chishti had given emperor Akbar his blessings in the 16th century, Akbar's Rajput princess, Jodhai Bai, produced an heir, thus ending his long period of childlessness. Ever since then hundreds have come to Salim Chishti's tomb to make a wish. The practice is to tie a thread on the marble screen around the tomb and hope for a miracle. Every day several new strings are tied to the screen, so the saint cannot be getting much eternal rest.

KEOLADEO GHANA NATIONAL PARK

Fifty five kilometres (34 miles) from Agra, the Bharatpur district is most famous for its Keoladeo Ghana National Park which includes a bird sanctuary. The town of Bharatpur was founded by Jat rulers in the 18th century. At its centre stands Lohagarh Fort (Iron Fort) which withstood many attacks from the bands of warriors who roamed this area after the decline of the Mughal empire.

The **Keoladeo Ghana National Park** in Bharatpur is a must-see. This once dry stony land was developed by Bharatpur rulers for use as a duck reserve. At the time duck shooting was a popular royal pastime – as many as 5000 birds could be shot in a single day. Today, the park is listed as a world heritage site and spreads over 29km² (11 square miles). It attracts over 300 bird species every year, including the Siberian crane, peregrine falcon, kingfisher, steppe eagle, different types of storks, herons and egrets. They can be seen crowding on islands in the water or flying out in a rush from the groves. Keoladeo has lovely walkways along the wetlands and bushes where the birds nest. You can either walk or cycle. There are also boats along the watercourses and cycle-rickshaws for hire. The park is open 06:00–18:00 daily, but the best time to see the birds is at dawn.

At the time of writing, Bharatpur has come under serious threat as a local water dispute is drying up the

Opposite: *The marble tomb of Sufi saint Chishti where wishes are granted.*
Left: *A nesting colony of painted stork at Keoladeo.*

INDIAN BIRDS

There is a dazzling array of birds in India and a pair of binoculars will always come in handy. Several species of birds can be seen at the Keoladeo Ghana National Park and in Delhi's zoo. Apart from parrots, parakeets, mynahs and peacocks, you can see the sarus crane, elephant bird and several varieties of cormorants. Along the countryside between Delhi and Agra you can occasionally see drongos and woodpeckers. Lapwings and tree pies are also common in Delhi and it is not unusual to find a peacock strutting in a Delhi park with its plumage unfurled. Kites are also very easily spotted when they swoop down over roofs and telephone wires. Vultures arrive in a flash if the carcass of a dog is not removed on time.

wetlands and the birds are moving elsewhere. Hopefully this dispute is settled before this magical place becomes a desert.

WATER PALACE AT DEEG

The tiny town of Deeg lies 98km (61 miles) north of Agra. It is not normally part of the tourist trail, but well worth a visit.

The rulers of Bharatpur loved the monsoon and the festivals associated with its dramatic arrival in northern India. The palace, built by the 18th-century ruler Raja Suraj Mal, is a breathtaking piece of architecture. It is an example of what is known as Monsoon Architecture – buildings designed to keep rooms cool by making use of the breeze and shutting out glare. The ingenious use of tanks, fountains and underwater cooling systems is exemplified by the palace at Deeg and shows how the architects dealt with the scorching heat of the Indian plains. The Water Palace overlooks two massive tanks, the Gopal Sagar and Rup Sagar. Water from these is diverted along waterways that are strategically placed throughout the palace complex. Nowadays the fountain jets on the waterways are only activated during the festival season. Two pavilions shaped like boats stretch out onto the main tank.

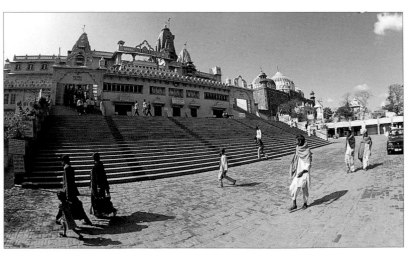

Left: *The Banyan (Indian Fig Tree) is a symbol of strength and endurance.* **Opposite:** *Hindu pilgrimage site in Mathura.*

MATHURA

Mathura, 62km (39 miles) from Agra, is the birthplace of Lord Krishna and as a result the surrounding towns are important centres of Hindu pilgrimage. The fact that these Hindu holy places continued to flourish right under the noses of the mighty Mughals who were proud Muslims, is a great tribute to the generally liberal policies of the emperors. This area is known as the *brajbhumi* and includes the towns of Vrindavan, Radhakund, Govardhan and Kosi.

Krishna, supposedly an incarnation of Vishnu, the Preserver, is one of the most popular Hindu gods. He is a blue skinned, flute-playing cow herder who slew the evil King Kamsa and brought peace to his land. He was also much loved by the local ladies. Krishna's birth is celebrated with an important festival called *Janmashtami*. It celebrates the birthday of Lord Krishna and takes place during the monsoon. It is best experienced in the temples of Vrindavan, 68km (42 miles) north of Agra. There is said to have been a fearsome rainstorm at Krishna's birth, to announce that 'the one who would destroy Kamsa' had been born. His father Vasudev carried baby Krishna across the Yamuna in a basket. The waters were so turbulent that Vasudev nearly drowned, but the great snake Sheshnag emerged from the river and spread its hood

---

INDIAN TREES

There is an immense variety of trees in India and although deforestation is a major problem, trees have often been the objects of worship. The Peepul tree is considered holy as the Buddha is supposed to have attained enlightenment while he was meditating under it. The Ashok tree is also an extremely popular Indian tree, shaped in a bulge at the top. Other common trees are Banyan, Neem and Jamun. The Banyan is a mighty tree with roots dangling from the branches. It is a symbol of all that is strong and enduring. The Neem is a medicinal tree and it is a common practice among Indians to use its branches to clean their teeth. The Jamun or blackberry tree is seen all over Delhi and Agra and yields a tangy dark fruit.

Above: *Dancing Nati's (goddess) relief in the Government Museum.*

over father and child to shelter them. Krishna was a naughty child, terribly fond of dairy products, particularly *ghee* and butter. Paintings of a chubby blue child wearing a feather crown and gorging on butter are extremely common in Hindu households and shops all over north India. Krishna's consort is the beautiful Radha, whom he wooed with the music of his flute. Love stories of Krishna and Radha have inspired many poems and legends. One of the most famous is the *Geet Govind*. Krishna's name is synonymous with love and sweet romance in lush green gardens. Famous is the rather grim looking room in the **Sri Krishna Janmabhoomi Temple** (on the outskirts of the city of Mathura) which marks the spot where Krishna was born. Mathura is a colourful, constantly festive city with temples lining its *ghats*. The most famous is **Vishram Ghat** where Krishna is said to have come after killing Kamsa.

The Krishna legend is by no means Mathura's only claim to fame. From the 5th century BC Mathura was a centre of Buddhism and regarded as the premier north Indian city in terms of its artistic and scholarly achievements. The Mathura school of art is on display at the **Government Museum** (open from 10:30 to 16:30, Tuesdays to Sundays). The museum has stone sculptures and brass artefacts dating from ancient Indian dynasties. It also houses the headless statute of Kanishka, a conqueror who founded a huge empire with its capital at Peshawar in the 1st century AD. There is also a statue of the Standing Buddha and fragments of ancient palaces. The images at the Government Museum show traces of Greek influence after Alexander's invasion of India. The museum as a whole provides glimpses of the rich north Indian civilisation over the last centuries BC through the first centuries AD.

VRINDAVAN

Vrindavan (Forest of Fragrant Basil) is where Krishna used to dance at Holi (the festival of colours) with Radha and her *gopis* (cowgirl consorts). The festival takes place between February and March and is celebrated on a full moon night towards the end of winter. People sprinkle coloured powder and water on each other, drink *bhang* (opium-flavoured milk), dance and sing. The town is an important Hindu pilgrimage site.

Of the many important temples located in Vrindavan, the most notable is **Govindeoji Temple** built in 1590 by Raja Man Singh I of Amber. This temple is seven storeys high and every year thousands of Vaishnavite pilgrims (followers of Vishnu) come here to pray. The **Sri Ranganathji Temple** is architecturally similar to the temples of south India. It has a carved *gopuram* (a pyramidical pillar) at its summit. During festivals, the temples of Vrindavan are decorated with flowers, clay lamps and brightly coloured flags.

Since the early decades of the 20th century, traditional Hindu families sent their widows to holy cities like Vrindavan and Benares. Some of them were extremely young because it was common practice to marry young girls to much older men. The widows shaved their heads and wore simple white clothes as a mark of their widowhood. The custom of sending widows to Vrindavan has almost completely disappeared today, although widows are still sent to this city from very poor areas because their families can no longer look after them. They live in the temples or in *vidhva ashrams* (widow shelters) and are cared for by the temple administrators. The plight of the widows of Vrindavan and Benares is a subject of great social concern and many citizen groups are campaigning for improved living conditions for them.

SIKANDRA

It is an irony that one of India's greatest kings is buried in a small village 8km (5 miles) from Agra. The tomb at Sikandra was completed by Jahangir and is built in the red sandstone favoured by Akbar. The mausoleum has no dome. Instead groups of *chhatris* are arranged along the roof. A *chhatri* with three arches, decorated with a profusion of intricate patterns in marble and black slate, towers above the massive arched gateway. The alcoves next to the main gateway perfectly match its shape. Sikandra must once have been very impressive. The garden around it is laid out according to the *charbagh* principles, and hordes of friendly monkeys come scrambling up for nuts.

Below: *The Ghat below Vishram Temple.*

GWALIOR

Only 119km (74 miles) south of Agra in the province of
Madhya Pradesh is the city of Gwalior which boasts,
among other things, of what is perhaps India's most fabulous hilltop fort. A little further south is sleepy Datia's
fascinating palace and Orchha's hidden mysteries. This is
a highly recommended detour which offers a concentrated dose of some of India's most spectacular
architecture. They are slightly off the beaten track but this
adds to their beguiling mystique. An extra day or two are
needed to make this trip from Agra.

Despite being dusty and crowded, Gwalior is home to
a major monument of Rajput genius and extravagance.
The spectacular hilltop fort, known as 'the pearl in the
necklace of the castles of Hindustan' is the finest of its
kind and has a long and turbulent history. Spreading over
a vast expanse of sandstone and comprising six palaces, it
is accessed by car or rickshaw from the west or through a
succession of gates in the northeast. The western road
snakes through a gorge and offers views to the curious Jain
rock sculptures. Enormous and solemn, these figures date
from between the seventh and the 15th centuries and
depict the 24 Jain teachers either sitting cross-legged with
palms turned upwards, or standing rigidly. Towering over
them is the 19m (62 feet) high sculpture of the Jain god
Adinath (with similar attributes to the Hindu god, *Shiva*).
There is a path leading up to the southeast entry of the
fort, where another cluster of sculptures is found and
where Jain worshippers leave offerings.

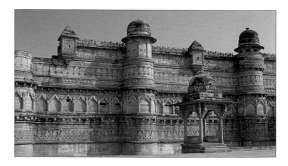

Opposite: *The detailed
cenotaphs at Orchha.*
Right: *Gwalior Fort: the
splendid façade of Man
Mandir or Painted Palace.*

The fort dates as far back as the 10th century when **Kachhawaha Rajputs** ruled the region. The Rajputs were, however, soon crushed by a Delhi sultan. Rather than face the invaders, the women of the fort committed mass suicide in a huge water tank north of the main palace, legendary for its medicinal waters. In the 14th century the **Tomars** established a new era of Rajput domination and a splendid new palace was erected under the powerful ruler **Man Singh** in the late 15th century. The main building of this palace, **Man Mandir** (Painted Palace), boasts of an exquisitely tiled exterior in turquoise, green and yellow, depicting exotic animals and palm trees. Other buildings and temples in the enclosure can be explored on foot. It is best to **hire a guide** for an hour or two, who can provide interesting historical details – but be sure to settle on payment beforehand.

DATIA

The magnificent seven-storeyed hilltop palace of Datia was built in the late 16th century by the eccentric Raja Bir Singh Deo, a friend of Prince Salim (later Jahangir). This is the other architectural wonder of India that was created by Lutyens, who also designed New Delhi. The fairytale palace offers fantastic views of the sleepy blue and white-washed village below. Giant stone elephants adorn its

---

VIOLENCE AT GWALIOR FORT

The magnificence of Gwalior Fort is all the more awe-inspiring for the violence of its history. When the Delhi sultan ousted the Rajputs in the 13th century, the royal ladies committed suicide and 700 prisoners were executed outside the sultan's tent. During the 16th century the Lodi sultans from Delhi once again attacked the Rajput fortress. Man Singh was captured and killed as was his son, who had heroically resisted the Muslims for a year. The eight wives of Man Singh, after beheading a succession of Muslim intruders at the doorways of their swing room (where the king had installed eight swings for them), committed suicide by fire.

Right: *The royal suite at Hotel Sheesh Mahal in Orchha.*

THE JAI VILAS PALACE

South of Gwalior fort, in an affluent part of the town, is the stupendous Jai Vilas Palace. It was built in the 19th century by the extremely rich Maharaja Jayaji Rao who belonged to a powerful Rajput clan, the Scindias, who had once been the masters of the fort. Determined to be on a par with his European counterparts, the raja sent a friend to Europe on a mission to collect the finest artefacts and ideas for a new residence. The result is this dazzlingly excessive hybrid of European architecture and furnishings, still inhabited by the Scindias but partly accessible to visitors. The palace contains curios like enormous multi-ton chandeliers, stuffed trophies from tiger hunts, and curiously, a collection of erotica.

top-storey façade, and a labyrinth of ascending passageways. *Jaali* screens and bright tilework lead up to the delicate apartments of the queen which still retain their exquisite murals. This is where the Raja liked to sit, close to his Rani, look out at the great plains of his kingdom and write poetry. There are no opening hours as such, but the caretaker lives outside the main entrance and allows visitors in as they arrive. He also provides an entertaining tour of the palace and idiosyncratic interpretations of Rajput history.

ORCHHA

This sleepy town, whose name means Hidden Place, casts a powerful spell on the visitor. The airy **Jahangir Mahal**, one of the most splendid palaces of Rajasthan, was built by local chief Raja Bir Singh Deo as a gift for a visiting allied emperor. Next door, the **Sheesh Mahal** (Mirror Palace) is a smaller palace doubling as a charming government-run hotel with breathtaking rooftop views. A must-see are the remarkably well-preserved frescoes from the *Ramayana* at the isolated Lakshminarayan Mandir, a 20-minute walk through town, as well as the dreamy *chhatris* by the river. Ask at the Sheesh Mahal for a **walkman-guided tour** of Orchha if you are only staying for a day.

Around Agra at a Glance

Oct–Mar is the best time to visit the Golden Triangle but in the Agra region it can be fairly hot even in Oct. **Dec–Jan** are preferable. Dec is also a good time to see Keoladeo Ghana National Park in Bharatpur. Maximum temperatures from **Nov–Feb** are 29°C (84°F) to 24°C (75°F); minimums are 12°C (54°F) to 10°C (50°F).

Roads around Agra are fairly well maintained, except for the dirt tracks leading to some of the smaller towns. The road to Bharatpur from the main highway is quite rocky and bumpy. Distances between Agra and the places around it are short and it is best to hire a taxi or chauffeur-driven vehicle, as the trauma of India's roads could test the hardiest driver. Most hotels have **chauffeur-driven tours** around the Agra region. Cars are not allowed within the park at Bharatpur; you can hire bicycles or cycle-rickshaws near the main gate and boats in the park. There are few taxis in the town, so to explore the surrounding area, it is best to organize a car from Agra.

Bharatpur
MID-RANGE
Laxmi Vilas Palace Hotel, Bharatpur, tel: (05644) 231 199; laxmivls@sancharnet.in A heritage hotel in a renovated Rajput palace. Enclosed court-yard, wild swans on its lawns and a pool. Mostly *Mughlai* food. Organizes excursions.
Bharatpur Forest Lodge, in the park, tel: (05644) 222 722/760, fax: (05644) 222 864. A comfortable hotel in the park, ready for birdwatching at dawn.

BUDGET
Hotel Sunbird, Bharatpur, tel: (05644) 225 701; hotel sunbird@gmail.com Clean but fairly basic hotel near the park, run by enthusiastic, knowledgeable bird-watchers. Other budget hotels near the park include the **Spoonbill Hotel**, tel: (05644) 226 981; **Falcon Guest House**, tel: (05644) 223 815; **Hotel Bharatpur Ashok**, tel: (05644) 222 760, 222 722.

Mathura
Best Western Radha Ashok, tel: (0565) 329 8427, fax: (0565) 253 0396. Best hotel in Mathura with air conditioning, friendly staff and a pool.
International Guest House, tel: (0565) 242 3888. Good value, serves vegetarian meals.

Vrindavan
MVT Guesthouse, tel: (0565) 254 0050; mvt@pamho.net Pretty gardens, good restaurant with pizza, cake and ice cream besides Indian food.
The ISKCON (International Society for Krishna Consciousness) **Guest House**, tel: (0565) 254 0021. Clean but spartan. Offers a good vegetarian *thali*.

Gwalior and Orchha
Usha Kiran Palace Hotel, Jayendraganj, Lakshar, Gwalior, tel: (0751) 244 4006; fax: (0751) 244 4018. Raj-style hotel, excellent restaurant.
The Sheesh Mahal, Orchha, tel: (07680) 252 624. A faded maharaja's palace, very good value for stunning rooms, good food in colonnaded hall and candle-lit rooftop dining.

Bharatpur offers painted miniatures of birds, available at the **Laxmi Vilas Palace Hotel**. In **Mathura** and **Vrindavan**, the markets are crowded with toys and *salwar kameez* (traditional Indian dress) sets. A large variety of delicious sweets is also available. Most popular is the *peitha* or candied pumpkin. You'll find incense, paintings, icons and replicas of temples.

Alwar Tourist Reception Centre, opp. railway station, tel: (0144) 21868.
Bharatpur Tourist Information Centre, opp. RTDC Hotel Saras, tel: (05644) 222 542.
Bharatpur Wildlife Office, Park Main Gate, National Highway 11, tel: (05644) 222777.
Gwalior, Madya Pradesh Tourism, Hotel Tansen (near station); tel: (0751) 234 0370.
Mathura Tourist Information Office, upstairs at old bus station; tel: (0565) 250 5351.
Orchha, Madya Pradesh Tourism, Hotel Sheesh Mahal.

Travel Tips

Tourist Information

There are tourist information offices run by central and state governments. For information, you may contact the overseas representatives of the Indian **Government Tourist Offices**. **Australia** (Sydney), tel: (02) 9221 9555, fax: (02) 9221 9777. **Canada** (Toronto), tel: (416) 962 3787, fax: (416) 962 6279. **Holland** (Amsterdam), tel: (020) 620 8991, fax: (020) 638 3059. **Singapore**, tel: (065) 6235 3800, fax: (065) 6235 8677. **South Africa**, tel: (011) 325 0880, fax: (011) 325 0882. **UK** (London), tel: (020) 7437 3677, fax: (020) 7494 1048. **USA** (Los Angeles), tel: (213) 380 8855, fax: (213) 380 6111; (New York), tel: (212) 586 4901-3, fax: (212) 582 3274. In Delhi, the **Government of India Tourist Office** HQ is 88 Janpath, Connaught Place, tel: (011) 2332 0005, or **Delhi Tourism Development Corporation**, N-36 Middle Circle, Connaught Place, tel: (011) 2331 3637. The **Rajasthan state tourist office** in Delhi is in Bikaner House, Pandara Road (south from India Gate), tel: (011) 2338 9525, and the **Uttar Pradesh office** in Chanderlok Building, 36 Janpath, tel: (011) 2332 2251. Also check the website

www.tourismindia.com
Embassies and High Commissions in Delhi:
Australia tel: (011) 4139 9900; **Canada** tel: (011) 4178 2000; **New Zealand** tel: (011) 2688 3170; **South Africa** tel: (011) 2614 9411-19; **UK** tel: (011) 2687 2161; **USA** tel: (011) 2419 8000.

Entry Requirements

You'll need a tourist visa which allows you to stay up to one, three or six months; The fee depends on the duration. Apply at your nearest Indian High Commission or Embassy with a travel itinerary and one or two passport photographs. If you're on a business trip, you will require a business visa, obtained in the same way. Allow at least a week for postal delivery, depending on location. Departure tax is Rs 750 (normally included in airfare).

Customs

On arrival in India, you must declare a sum exceeding US $10,000 or any valuables, such as video cameras and laptops. Travellers over the age of 17 can import one bottle of wine and 250ml spirits, 200 cigarettes, 50 cigars, or 250g of tobacco. You can export handicrafts, but there are restrictions on antiques. It is illegal to export objects made from animal skin or ivory.

Health Requirements

Although you need no health certificate to enter India, immunization prior to travel is essential, as is travel insurance. The basic vaccines are for typhoid, meningitis, hepatitis A, tetanus, diptheria and polio. A rabies jab is advisable only if you will be working with animals. Malaria, transmitted by mosquitoes, is widespread in India, especially during the monsoon season (July–August). Consult a doctor about the latest malaria tablets and remember to continue taking the tablets for four weeks after your trip, as malaria has an incubation period of a month.

Getting There

By air: New agreements signed in 2005 have paved the way for greatly increased air services between India, the UK and the USA, including direct flights to many regional airports. Meantime Air India, British Airways and Virgin operate regular non-stop flights to Delhi. Prices can be brought down considerably by stopping en route.

Amongst the cheapest options is Etihad, via Abu Dhabi. UK tel: (020) 8735 6700; Delhi tel: (011) 3901 3901; website: www.etihadairways.com

By road: The road from Europe passes through Turkey, Iran and Pakistan. Alternatively, you may take the Trans-Siberian Express to China and then travel southwest to India.

What to Pack

Light, loose-fitting cotton clothing and **comfortable** footwear is essential. You may prefer closed sports shoes instead of sandals due to the dirt and dust on the streets. Avoid walking barefoot outdoors, unless you have to when visiting temples. Indians dress **conservatively**, especially women, and bare arms and legs, as well as tight pants, will attract stares. For both men and women, shorts should be a last resort. When entering temples, mosques and Muslim quarters, cover your legs and arms. Bring light winter clothing for the November–February period when it can be chilly, especially at night. Pack a raincoat for the monsoon months. For formal occasions and social gatherings, dress smartly – Indians are appearance-conscious and dress beautifully. Pack light, as you are likely to have excess baggage after visiting all the interesting shops.

Money Matters

The monetary unit is the rupee (Rs). There are a hundred paise in a rupee. You will mostly deal with banknotes, though there are coins too: 25 paise, 50 paise, and 1, 2 and 5 rupees. Try to keep small change on you, as getting change back can be a hassle.

Currency exchange: The easiest currency to convert is US dollars, followed by the pound sterling. Travellers' cheques are safer than cash, and are generally accepted by **Thomas Cook** and **American Express** – provided they are in US dollars or pounds. To change cash, Thomas Cook, American Express or your hotel are hasslefree opportunities, and should take most currencies. There are plenty of ATMs with 24-hour access that take foreign cards.

Credit cards: Mastercard, Visa, American Express and Diners Club are accepted in most hotels, restaurants and shopping emporia. You can also pay for train tickets by credit card.

Tipping: *Baksheesh* is much practised. You are expected to tip porters, waiters, hotel staff and anyone else who delivers a satisfactory service. Ten rupees is the minimum but it is really up to you how much to give. Locals give beggars alms and joining in is the decent and appreciated thing to do.

Tax: Tax varies, but expect a 10 per cent tax on your hotel bill. You can always inquire before you check in and try to negotiate a better deal.

Accommodation

The hotels recommended in this book are mostly mid- to top-range. Cheaper establishments have obvious disadvantages (lack of air conditioning, shared facilities and poor hygiene). Some hotels have air coolers that also do the trick. Most medium-priced hotels have reasonable in-house restaurants and room service. The main difference between mid- and top-range rooms, aside from the décor, is the mosquitoes – but this need only be a concern during the monsoon season (May–September). There are two types of top-range hotels. First, the Raj-style 'heritage' hotels – usually converted medieval palaces and *haveli*. The second type is the modern luxury hotel, often an international chain such as Oberoi, Meridien, Ashok and Claridges. The Taj Group of Hotels seek to emulate a Raj authenticity but are more business-like, although their grandeur is impressive. Most deluxe hotels have several top restaurants, a beauty salon, shops, pool, gym and a booking information service for tourists. Some even have good bakeries. Book in advance because the Golden Triangle attracts Indian as well as foreign visitors at all times.

Eating Out

In India, you can eat very well on a small budget and lavishly on a large one. This part of India has an astonishing variety of foods, among which the heavy and exotic Mughlai cuisine, and of course, northern Indian food.

GOOD READING

- *India Magazine*, cultural monthly.
- **G Barton & L Malone** (1988), *Old Delhi: 10 Easy Walks*, Delhi.
- **W Dalrymple**, *City of Djinns*, London (highly readable account of a year spent in Delhi).
- **P Davies** (1989), *Penguin Guide to the Monuments of India*, Volume I & II, London.
- **G Devi** (1976), *A Princess Remembers: the Memoirs of the Maharani of Jaipur*, London.
- **R E Frykenberg** (1986), *Delhi Through the Ages*, New Delhi.
- **Kushwant Singh**, (1990), *Delhi: a Novel*.
- **V S Naipaul** (1990), *A Million Mutinies Now*, London (classic overview of Indian society, highly recommended).
- **M Tully** (1991), *No Full Stops in India*, London (BBC journalist's account of modern India).

Indian food of all kinds, but especially the wonderful and light South Indian dishes, is available in establishments ranging from very cheap and safe popular eateries to luxury hotel restaurants. Delhi is a gourmet's paradise and in addition to Asian and European cuisines, it has many Western-style fast-food establishments like *Pizza Hut* and *McDonalds*. Jaipur has a selection of restaurants, though authentic Rajasthani food is not easy to come by. Agra is sadly lacking in this department – there are a number of good restaurants but not nearly enough to cater for the demand. Most of Delhi's finest restaurants are in luxury hotels and in the residential districts of New Delhi.

Transport

Air: Air travel is ideal for those with very limited time, but it foregoes the wonderful experience of seeing the countryside that land travel provides. There are regular flights from Delhi to both Agra and Jaipur with **Indian Airlines** (see page 58); and **Jet Airways** (see page 78). The domestic airport is 15km (9 miles) southwest of the city; Enquiries, tel: (011) 2569 6021, 2566 1000 (domestic), 2560 2000 (international)

Road: Exploring the Golden Triangle by car is definitely the best way to do it. There are two options: hiring a self-drive car or a chauffeur-driven vehicle. The first is slightly cheaper and can be done through any of the international companies like **Hertz** or **Budget**, or through a travel agent or tourist office. This option is not recommended, however, Indian roads are dangerous and have a high death toll. The second, safer, option involves taking a driver along, who might offer further insights into some of the things you come across on your trip. Book through a tourist office, travel agent, or at your hotel. **Rajasthan Tourism Development Corporation**, Bikaner House, Pandara Rd,

tel: (011) 2338 3837.

Buses: Buses are a good, safe substitute for a car. Although there are state-run buses, if comfort is a priority use the luxury buses run by private companies and hotels. Book through any travel agent (see above) or at your hotel.

Trains: Trains are efficient, even if crowded, and are recommended for long-distance travel. They are also a fast way to get around the Golden Triangle if you don't want to stop on the way; ideal for direct trips from Delhi to Jaipur and Agra. The best train journeys are: **Delhi-Agra** on the Shatabdi Express, departs 06:15 arrives 08:12, departs 18:40 arrives 21:45. **Agra-Delhi** on the Shatabdi Express, departs 20:30 arrives 22:30. **Delhi-Jaipur** on the Shatabdi Express (Ajmer Shatabdi), departs 06:10 arrives 10:45. **Haridwar-Ahmedabad** (Ahmedabad Mail), departs 22:50 arrives 04:30. For overnight journeys, book a second- or first-class sleeping wagon.

There are three main railway stations – **New Delhi Station**, **Delhi Station** in Old Delhi and **Hazrat Nizamuddin**. For bookings, tel: 1330/35/45, www.indianrail.gov.in

Book second or first class. The famous trip in the **Palace on Wheels** is in its own class. It departs every week from Delhi, and goes through Jaipur, Udaipur, Jaisalmer, Jodhpur, Bharatpur and Agra. Prices are hefty, but the itinerary is exceptional. For bookings, UK tel: (0125) 858 0600; USA toll free: 877 463 4299;

e-mail: bookings@palaceon
wheels.net; website: www.
palaceonwheels.net

Taxis: Taxis are cheap and
readily available. In Delhi and
Jaipur they are painted black
and yellow. In congested traffic, auto rickshaws are faster
and even cheaper, although
you get more of the pollution.
Cycle rickshaws are unstable in
traffic, but a splendid way to
see the narrow streets of Old
Agra and Old Delhi. This experience is compulsory – and
safe. Negotiate payment before
you set off, or have the driver
turn on the meter. You should
tip the cycle-rickshaw driver.

Business Hours

Shops: Shops are open 09:30–
18:00, Monday–Saturday. Markets have longer hours. On
Sunday shops and most markets are closed. Some shops
have individual trading hours.
Offices: Government tourist
offices open from
09:30–17:00, Monday–Friday
and from 09:30–13:00
Saturday. Saturday is
a working day in India.
Pharmacies: There are 24-
hour pharmacies in most
cities. Ask at your hotel.
Post Offices: From 10:00–
17:00, Monday–Friday and
until noon on Saturday.

Time

All of India is five and a half
hours ahead of Greenwich
Mean Time.

Communications

Telephones: The international
code for India is 91, followed
by the local code (with a zero

CONVERSION CHART		
FROM	**TO**	**MULTIPLY BY**
Millimetres	Inches	0.0394
Centimetres	Inches	0.3937
Metres	Yards	1.0936
Metres	Feet	3.281
Kilometres	Miles	0.6214
Square kilometres	Square miles	0.386
Hectares	Acres	2.471
Litres	Pints	1.760
Kilograms	Pounds	2.205
Tonnes	Tons	0.984
To convert Celsius to Fahrenheit: x 9 ÷ 5 + 32		

for national calls) – 11 for
Delhi, 141 for Jaipur, and 562
for Agra. You can make direct
or operator-assisted calls to
any country. Collect and
credit card calls to some coun-
tries such as the USA, UK,
Ireland, Canada, Australia,
New Zealand among others
are possible. In cities, you will
see STD booths (Standard
Trunk Dialling) where you can
call any national or international destination for a fee
considerably smaller than at
your hotel – it is calculated by
the second. Some booths are
open night and day. Most
hotels have fax facilities, as do
the STD booths. GSM mobile
phones work and coverage is
excellent. Visitors from North
America will need a tri band
phone.
Post: Post to and from India is
generally reliable but it can
be slow. Buy your stamps at
the post office and hand your
mail over the counter rather
than put it in a letterbox.
Sending a parcel is a convo-
luted affair – parcels have to
be stitched into cotton cloth,
wax-sealed, custom-cleared,

and are best registered. This
can be done for you at larger
post offices. Printed matter
can be sent more cheaply as
'book post'. For speed, use a
courier firm.
Media: There are some good-
quality English-language newspapers; among these are: *The
Hindu, Times of India, The
Independent* and *The Indian
Express*. Magazines of substance are *India Today,
Outlook* and *The India
Magazine* (cultural events).

Electricity

Power supply is 220V, 50Hz.
For sensitive appliances, use
a stabilizer (available at larger
hotels). The plugs are
European-style with three
round pins (two-pin plugs
are fine too).

Weights and Measures

The metric system is used.
Gold and silver are sold by
11.5 grams, or *tola*. Precious
stones are weighed in carats
(0.2g). In Statistics *lakhs* and
crores are used. A *lakh* is
100,000 units and a *crore* is
100 *lakhs*.

Health Precautions

It is advisable to pack a survival kit consisting of electrolyte powder that also guards against dehydration in summer; antibiotics; aspirin; throat lozenges; allergy medication; antiseptic cream; band-aids; insect repellent, sun-block, antibacterial towels and gel.

Visitors to India may experience short-term intestinal trouble, also known as **Delhi-belly**, due to the novelty of the food and water, combined with the heat. But if you take the following precautions, you should be fine: for the first few days eat simple food such as South Indian *thali* (platter), yoghurt, bread and rice. **Tap water** is unsafe. Drink only mineral or filtered water (sold at street kiosks in hotels and restaurants) and bottled soft drinks. Check the seal on mineral water bottles. Brush your teeth with mineral or filtered water too. Avoid ice cubes in your drinks. Steer clear of fresh vegetables, salads and cut fruit. Peel uncut fruit. Avoid street vendors – eat in restaurants and cafés where the food is freshly cooked. Avoid seafood. To ward off heat exhaustion, drink plenty of fluids, use sun-block and wear a hat. If you do succumb to the heat, rest in a cool room and drink lots of fluids. To prevent heat rash use talcum powder and wear loose-fitting cotton clothing. Avoid mosquitoes if possible – wear insect-repellent, especially in the evenings, and cover your legs and arms. In Delhi, mosquitoes don't generally carry malaria outside the monsoon season. During the monsoon and outside of Delhi however, take malaria pills. Stay away from dogs, monkeys and cattle. Wash your hands frequently – if water is unavailable on the road or while sightseeing, use antibacterial towels or antibacterial gel.

Health Services

If you need a doctor, enquire at your hotel.

Hospitals: All-India Institute of Medical Sciences (AIIMS), Ansari Nagar, Sri Aurobindo Marg, New Delhi, tel: (011) 2658 8500, 2659 4404. Open 24 hours. SMS Hospital, Sawai Ram Singh Marg, Jaipur, tel: (0141) 256 0291. District Hospital, MG Road, Agra, tel: (0562) 246 3043, 2455 099.

Safety

You are unlikely to be pick-pocketed in Delhi or Jaipur, though try not to carry large amounts of cash on you and leave your passport in the hotel. Women are safe but should keep their legs and shoulders covered.

Emergencies

Police, tel: 100 (national). Also ask at your hotel.

Etiquette

Remove your shoes before entering a temple or mosque, as well as some private homes. In mosques, if admitted, women cover their heads. Use your right hand for eating, shaking hands or pointing, as Indians use the left hand to wash in the lavatory. Ask people before photographing them, as some dislike it. Some Muslim women cover their faces when photographed or turn their backs. Check before taking photos inside places of worship. Public displays of intimacy between men and women are not acceptable in Indian society.

Language

There are 15 official languages in India, of which Hindi, English and Urdu are most common. In urban areas most people speak at least basic English, but this is not the case in the countryside and in provincial towns. A few words of Hindi will take you a long way.

USEFUL HINDI PHRASES

namaste • **greetings, hello**
dhanyavaad • **thank you**
kitna hai • **how much**
davai ki dukaan • **medicine shop**
paani • **water**
teekha • **hot (as in chilli)**
nahin chahiye • **I don't want**
maaph kijiye • **sorry**
kidhar hai • **where is it**
khana • **food**
garam • **hot (as in oven)**
thanda • **cold**
theek hai • **okay**
kal • **tomorrow**
parso • **day after tomorrow**
jaao • **go away**
nahin • **no**
achcha • **nice**
achcha laga • **I liked it**
ganda • **dirty**
han • **yes**

INDEX

Note: Numbers in **bold**
indicate photographs